MW01289242

JOURNEY
TO
MUDRYI

JOURNEY TO MUDRYI

THE WISDOM THAT UNDERLIES ALL HEALING

IRA KAMP, DDS

JOURNEY TO MUDRYI
THE WISDOM THAT UNDERLIES ALL HEALING

Copyright © 2017 Ira Kamp.

All rights reserved. No part of this book may be used or reproduced by any means, graphic, electronic, or mechanical, including photocopying, recording, taping or by any information storage retrieval system without the written permission of the author except in the case of brief quotations embodied in critical articles and reviews.

iUniverse books may be ordered through booksellers or by contacting:

iUniverse
1663 Liberty Drive
Bloomington, IN 47403
www.iuniverse.com
1-800-Authors (1-800-288-4677)

Because of the dynamic nature of the Internet, any web addresses or links contained in this book may have changed since publication and may no longer be valid. The views expressed in this work are solely those of the author and do not necessarily reflect the views of the publisher, and the publisher hereby disclaims any responsibility for them.

Any people depicted in stock imagery provided by Thinkstock are models, and such images are being used for illustrative purposes only. Certain stock imagery © Thinkstock.

ISBN: 978-1-5320-1575-5 (sc)
ISBN: 978-1-5320-1574-8 (e)

Library of Congress Control Number: 2017902914

Print information available on the last page.

iUniverse rev. date: 06/28/2017

Be realistic; plan for a miracle.
—Osho

CONTENTS

ACKNOWLEDGMENTS

Marne O'Shae	For being a constant inspiration in my life and work
Margaret McCasland	For her hours of diligent editing
Helen Bayer	For her compassionate wisdom in editing
Hilda Moleski	For her inspired editing
Rachel Clark	My daughter, for tolerating my adventures in her life
Reuben Kamp	My son, for tolerating my adventures in his life
Ruth Moleski	For seeing the divine in my work
Marcia Margolan	For creating the possibility of science and intuition
Ralph Alan Dale	For showing me the way of simplicity and magic in acupuncture
Dr. Maurice Tischler	For inspiring me to pursue homeopathy and acupuncture

Steven and Marcia	My brother and sister, for showing me the power of wishes
Vladimir Bobkoff	For our many years of friendship and for giving me Mudryi
Laure Kamp	For her inspiration in meditation and our children
R. A. Flickinger	For giving me the opportunity to see spirit in science
Rusti	For giving me the inspirational walks in the woods
Alan Shernoff	For his guidance in being a man
Mabel Beggs	For her inspiration into the world of soul and spirit
Kate Payne	For her steadfastness in keeping the world of spirit alive
Trina Kamp	For her spiritual guidance
Florence and George	For giving me my life and imagination
Dianne Lynn	For her many years of love and inspiring illustrations
Kelly Ryan	For her poetry in healing
Meagan and Naani	For keeping the possibility of family alive

FOREWORD

*Now you're working on building a mystery and
choosing so carefully holding on, holding in.*
—*Sarah McLachlan*

What does it mean to work in a healing environment?
From what are we healing? How do we know or feel or
sense a shift in ourselves that confirms that healing has
taken place?

There are more questions than answers in a field that
has a unique form of empirical data. Much of what lies
beneath a healing process is a sensed experience and quite
personal. These sensations or observations may be subtle,
but as we practice noticing these subtle shifts, the effects
can be profound.

Healing is a natural part of having a body. Healing is
what I am interested in exploring, as well as its relationship
to that which is spiritual. Maybe it is not the definition
of healing that I seek but its relationship to my spirit and
how to integrate these ideas.

I come to these questions at the moment because I was
invited to work as a licensed massage therapist at Dr.

Kamp's dental office and continued in that position for nearly six years. I learned and experienced fascinating things while I was there. I would say at the core of those experiences was the realization that we all are part of creating a field, a shared space where what we do and feel has an impact on the whole room.

It seems important to share that it took a couple of years to really create a rhythm with the whole staff and feel like what I was offering there was, in fact, "healing" more than it was a mere massage.

In the beginning, Dr. Kamp would give his patients the option, simply asking, "Would you like a massage?" Later, we warmed up to the idea that I was not just there as a complimentary service but was there to create and shift the feeling of the room entirely. This caused Dr. Kamp to say to his patients, "Kellie is here today, and her being here helps me. How about if she comes in to offer massage?" Sometimes he would just have me come in, and he'd say, "Kellie is here; she is going to work on your feet while I am treating you."

Well, this changed the number of yeses we received and gave Dr. Kamp and me a shared intention: we were in there to get a dental procedure done well and with integrity. Our shared intention included my being there. This made a difference in the way it impacted the patients, but more so, it aligned me with Dr. Kamp. An invitation to be part of something is like a door swinging open and having an effect on the entire scene. Without this invitation, it was just a crapshoot of whether or not the client was open to massage. Dr. Kamp supported a healing environment by saying he was a direct recipient of it. He clearly stated that my being in the room had an impact on him as he worked on the patient. What I brought to the room was a stillness and presence and calm that directly affected the patient and therefore affected Dr. Kamp. Everyone received what I offered to the room. Not dissimilarly, the patient and the dentist and the assistants all had an impact on me and on each other. I suppose that is my point: we all have the potential to create a new experience in the room during any procedure, situation, or circumstance within the shared space. Why did Dr. Kamp feel that my focus and attention on the patient would benefit him? What made the environment so different? What was transforming in the room? Seemingly, the most assertive part of healing is the concept and actualization of intention. Intention to bring a healing presence into a room will likely change the quality of feeling in the room. It's simple, not to be mistaken for control. I don't know what will happen or how, but if I *intend* a way of being (i.e., present, gregarious, open, gentle), then I can contribute that part to the whole of the room. If the patient is stressed and upset, and the dental assistant is impatient, and the dentist is upset about something, then my contribution may not dominate, but it still can have an effect. In fact, the more I stick to the intention, the more likely it will be to fill up space and change the energy and the comfort level in the room.

Giving and receiving are just a breath away from one another. My giving may not be received by the other bodies in the room. One has to be aware, to some extent, of what is possible in order to make room for receiving it.

This is why a shared intention multiplies the potential for actualization. When Dr. Kamp shared with the patient the idea of my coming into the room for the benefit of his own work on the patient, it strengthened the collective consciousness. He was doubling my intention by inviting me in for his benefit and then tripling it when he shared this intention with the patient. By the time I sat down to give massage, there was already an outlet for receiving the healing touch, just by Dr. Kamp's speaking the intention.

This is true of so many things in life, and it is a wonderful thing to practice as a way of feeling like you are participating in a much greater web of the universe. It is easy in our culture today to be individualized and feel separate. We are under the impression that we ought to do it ourselves and achieve self-worth through achievements and accomplishments. So much of what we crave is connection and love. Through the understanding that we are part of something greater, we may feel that connection. This "something greater" could be as simple as shared intention. It is the fuel behind what makes things happen. Intention also can bring change. When we share our intentions with others, we give them the opportunity to see something that they might not have seen before. If we can't imagine it, then we likely cannot make it happen. If we can imagine it, then let's intend it and see then what happens. There is only so much that we can leave to mystery.

I think it is somehow in the mystery that we really come to life. Somehow for the healer types, it is more interesting to live in the questions than in the answers. Maybe this is what divides us from the health professionals who are grounded by science and research.

The mystery too lives in the synchronicity of the Sarah McLachlan song "Building a Mystery," which I quoted at the beginning of this passage and which is playing in the background as I write this. It's beautiful to think that something greater than we are yet potentially made up of all our intentions somehow reflects back to us in the vast, mysterious universe.

Kellie Ryan, LMT

IN THE BEGINNING

I have always been attracted to magic, though not the kind that fools our senses through sleight of hand or smoke and mirrors. What fascinates me is the magic of human life. The workings of our physical bodies, the energy that lies beneath our physical natures, the stormy weather created by our emotions, and the creative processes of our minds are all manifestations of real magic.

On my journey, I discovered that meditation connects my intellect with my soul. In turn, my soul guides my intellect in healing. The role of meditation in healing cannot be understated. When I connect with my soul through meditation, an intimate relationship is formed that benefits both healer and the person receiving healing. *Journey to Mudryi* (Moo´dray) tells the story of my journey through a world where wisdom seemed concealed behind a veil. My tale is like a quest where the traveler does not know what is at the end of the journey but continues on, as something magical is calling. Later, I came to know that this quest to find the meaning of life through the eyes of a healer was the calling of my soul.

Over the past two centuries, science and empirical

thinking have led us away from recognizing and acknowledging other states of consciousness. I am grateful for the musicians, artists, poets, philosophers, and enlightened writers of past generations who have kept alive our hearts when our analytical minds have tried to dominate our lives.

The universe is one huge force field in which we swim, interacting with all sorts of forces and energy flows. We can sense some of these forces with our sight, hearing, feeling, taste, and smell; others we can only sense through intuition, our sixth sense. The landscape of the earth and other celestial bodies, radio waves, microwaves, emotions, mental energy, cosmic rays, sunshine, and karma and the divine energy, as well as our physical bodies, are the architecture of our consciousness. As organic entities, we interact, create, destroy, and transform energy. Our energy field is a canvas on which we leave our imprint, creating landscapes, dramas, and portraits of our own choosing.

Journey to Mudryi was written as a resource for practitioners of all healing modalities, as well as for people in need of healing. I invite you to put yourself in a skeptic's shoes, whether you are a practitioner of conventional medicine or an alternative healer. The journey will lead you to an understanding of energetic healing that has never been presented before. *Energetic healing* is used here as a term for any therapy that treats the energy that runs through our bodies to achieve balance and healing. Whether you are an existing practitioner with a discipline or an emerging practitioner, becoming aware and utilizing co-cognition will enhance your practice. Co-cognition is an unconscious aspect of healing, and a health care practitioner can become aware of its presence. This book was written for three kinds of healers:

> ➢ You want to be a healer but do not yet have a discipline.
> ➢ You are practicing in a traditional setting, such as medicine or nursing, and would like to incorporate co-cognition.
> ➢ You are practicing in an alternative setting and would like to incorporate co-cognition.

You will discover and experience the three keys to healing—*co-cognition*, *compassion*, and *Mudryi*. Co-cognition, I discovered, is a most important attribute of our souls. There is a place where souls communicate and share information. I have named this sharing between souls *co-cognition*. It is a place where both healer and patient communicate—often unconsciously until we become aware of its possibility. Co-cognition is an ongoing process in our healing relationships; co-cognition can be brought to awareness with study, understanding, and the practice of meditation. Co-cognitive healing is bringing co-cognition into the practice of healing.

Can you bring peace to and be blameless in your listening for others? Can you create empathy, fellow feeling, care, concern, sensitivity, warmth, love, tenderness, mercy, leniency, tolerance, kindness, and humanity? Developing a compassionate mind brings these, as well as tolerance, acceptance, and clarity, to the healing relationship. Compassion facilitates co-cognition by creating a presence of calmness so that clear communication can occur.

Joining your compassionate mind and co-cognition in your healing work opens a door—a door to soul consciousness. The seat of knowledge and wisdom that lies within soul consciousness I have named *Mudryi*. I looked for a word that would refer to the wisdom within a patient who is suffering or sick. I could find no such word in the English language. A Russian colleague and friend, Dr. Vladimir Bobkoff, introduced me to the Russian word *Mudryi*, which means a person who is wise even in the midst of suffering. I felt the connection to this word.

Those of us in the healing professions tend to see illness as a misfortune, many times preventable. What we don't see is the wisdom that lies under the suffering. It is like looking at a three-dimensional picture, where initially only dots and lines are seen. Then, with enough patience and focus, the picture comes out. We can see a patient as lots of dots, but seeing a patient as Mudryi is seeing the picture behind the dots.

Over time, I came to know that Mudryi exists in all of us and that in the context of healing, Mudryi holds the wisdom that is in the soul of the patient. By learning to listen to Mudryi in our patients, we can be empowered in healing.

Much of my work in preparation for this book has been done in conjunction with the Foundation of Light in Ithaca, New York. The Foundation of Light and its founders have been an important resource for my work and life. In 1974, several people, including John Payne, Kate Payne, and Mabel Beggs, started the Foundation of Light with the intent of creating a holistic learning community and a spiritual center for meditation, healing, and study. The Foundation of Light promotes spiritual understanding and practices as found in all the world's great religions, in accordance with divine purpose or cosmic law. Programs at the foundation include the study and practice of meditation and spiritual healing, investigations into different levels of awareness or consciousness, the influence of natural foods in promoting health, the impact of thought and visualization in bringing about spiritual growth, the development of individual creativity, and the advancement of world peace and unity.

I first met John, Kate, and Mabel in 1986, when they were all in their seventies. They spoke of life in a way that I had never heard before: reincarnation, guides, angels, and healing energies, as if the world is really full of magic. Until this point, I had only noticed complaints and conflicted relationships among the older generation. The elders in my originating family had seemed to be lacking a dimension of life. The elders at the Foundation of Light were like a breath of fresh air.

I took over the position of facilitator for the healing group at the Foundation of Light in 1993. I had previously been to a few meetings but knew very little about what went on in the group. I went into the group thinking I knew a lot, for I had training in acupuncture, homeopathy, craniosacral therapy, and nutrition. However, I found my training meant little when true healing occurred.

People who had little or no training were as effective as professionals. My experiences in the healing group have transformed my paradigm of healing. To this day, I am grateful for the opportunities that the Foundation of Light has given me.

The lives and works of Alice Bailey, Buddha, Carl Jung, and the Theosophists also have helped me bring forth the ideas and practice of co-cognition in healing. I have used co-cognitive healing in my work for the past twenty-five years. I developed this system of healing while searching for what underlies all forms of healing. Connecting with patients in this manner is invaluable for me and my patients. All of us heal better in a calm and supportive environment, and co-cognition creates this environment.

Alice A. Bailey (1880–1949) wrote many books about esoteric nature, healing, and spiritual life. Her works were a major resource for this book. She identified herself as a "rabid orthodox Christian worker who became a well-known occult teacher." She laid the groundwork for people practicing energetic or spiritual healing all over the planet. Alice Bailey developed a worldview and "an absolute conviction that one divine Life pervades and animates the one humanity."[1]

Buddha (563–483 BCE) was born Siddhartha Gautama, an Indian prince who became one of the greatest religious teachers of the world. Buddha's writings and teachings lay the foundation for living a life of compassion, an essential component of healing.

Carl Jung (1875–1961) was a Swiss psychologist and

early colleague of Freud's who broke from Freudian analysis when he founded the school of analytical psychology. Jung's work underlies many of the modern models of psychology and spirituality—he integrated psychology and spirituality. Using Jung's ideas, I understood that there is a spiritual connection between my patients and me, like a telephone line, by which we can talk to each other, but there is no speaking. Co-cognition arose from this idea. I associate my nonverbal communication with what Jung calls *synchronicity*—something happens that is important but has no apparent cause. But there is a cause; we just don't recognize it. My experience with synchronicity is that when I focus, I can tune into the spiritual nature of my patient. I now know, with the focus of my attention, there is synchronicity between my mind and everything else. Co-cognition is based on this experience; that there is a synchronicity between the minds of the healer and the patient.

Theosophy is a spiritual movement that brought Eastern spiritual concepts such as Buddhism to the West during the late 1800s in a form that could be understood by Western cultures. Helena Blavatsky, born to a noble Russian family, was trained by Tibetan Buddhist masters from 1868 to 1870. Blavatsky gave the name *Theosophy*, which means literally "knowledge of the divine," to the concepts she brought from the Tibetan masters. From 1875 until her death in 1891, she spread Theosophy around the world, where it has maintained a following into the twenty-first century.

Certain ways of healing existed way before the advent

of science—alternative, complementary, and spiritually based healing. Many of these ways are still found in today's world and are practiced apart from science-based medicine. I believe there is a great need for integrating spiritually based healing with medicine and surgery. While myriad books have been written on energetic and spiritual healing, this book brings all forms of healing together into one context. Whether or not you have formal training and experience in the healing arts, I invite you to develop your ability to heal. This book shares information on energetic healing that will be useful for practitioners of energetic healing, such as acupuncturists, massage therapists, naturopaths, chiropractors, spiritual counselors, and healers, as well as more typical Western practitioners, such as physicians, nurses, and psychologists. It is my hope that this book will allow readers of all persuasions of thought around healing to better understand and move forward in creating a healing experience that is effective, tolerant, and respectful of each person's path on his or her journey to transformation.

Since my journey to Mudryi, my experiences in teaching healing to other people have reinforced the basic keys to healing:

➢ Healing energy is basic to all of us, unrelated to the amount of formal training we have received or the experiences we have encountered. In healing workshops at the Foundation of Light, the quality of healing has not been related to the healer's prior experience or training. As a unique form of healing was introduced to new receivers and healers, we saw that even novices could be healers. Co-cognition also enhanced the work of experienced healers, no matter what technique they had training in.

➤ Healing energy originates in the soul. As healing practitioners, our skills and knowledge serve as great tools for delivering healing. However, no matter which healing modalities we use (surgery, medicine, dentistry, psychotherapy, acupuncture, homeopathy, alternative, spiritual healing, etc.), the source of our healing energy lies within our souls.

➤ Soul communication enhances healing. The compassionate intention of the healer and the will of the recipient to heal inspire their communication. The healer's compassion for the receiver replaces the need to figure out what is wrong with the person. The healer then uses his or her intuition and intellect to transform the wisdom of Mudryi into whatever form of healing he or she can best use to benefit the person who is suffering.

➤ Osho, a twentieth-century spiritual and psychological guide says that love is the ultimate path to healing.

Love is the most healing force in the world; nothing goes deeper than love. It heals not only the body, not only the mind, but also the soul. If one can love, then all one's wounds disappear. Then one becomes whole—and to be whole is to be holy.

Unless one is whole one is not holy. The physical health is a superficial phenomenon. It can happen through medicine; it can happen through science. But the innermost core of one's being can be healed only through love. Those who know the secret of love know the greatest secret of life. Then there is no misery for them, no old age, no death. Of course, the body will become old and the body will die, but love reveals to you the truth that you are not the body. You are pure consciousness, you have no birth, no death. And to live in that pure consciousness is to live in tune with life. Bliss is a by-product of living in tune with life.[2]

By opening to love, to the wisdom of our souls, and to the wisdom of those who suffer, these keys help us relieve their suffering and enlighten us as conscious beings. The wisdom of Mudryi, plus the compassionate mind and the enlightened intuition of the healer, unlock doors that have contained our suffering for generations. I invite you to pick up the keys and unlock your doors.

I am full of gratitude for my wife, Dr. Marne O'Shae, and my children, Rachel and Reuben, for their patience and willingness to accept my work in their lives.

Ira Kamp, DDS, certified acupuncturist
Ithaca, New York

INTRODUCTION

*In the beginning, in the middle, and in the end,
it was there; I just didn't notice. "Who are you?"
I asked. "Mudryi," came the answer.*

I am a dentist and a New York State–certified acupuncturist, practicing in Ithaca, New York. As a young man, I graduated dental school and received my acupuncture certification. You may be wondering why a dentist would be interested in methods of healing other than dentistry. Well, for much of my life, I have had a desire to understand healing. From an early age, I felt sympathy for those who were sick. I was inspired by a family member who was a dentist to choose dentistry as a profession. My real motivation, however, was to be involved with healing people, and dentistry was a way into this. My inspiration for healing came from many sources, including myself. This is one of my experiences along the way.

When I was forty-four, I had a heart attack while playing hockey. It was not severe, but the experience was still a journey I had to go through. A small branch of one of my coronary arteries was clogged. At the time, I joked that my artery was filled with tofu because I was a vegetarian. After the hockey game, I drove myself to the hospital and was eventually released with a diagnosis of indigestion. The hospital actually missed the fact that I indeed had a heart attack. Two days later, I again experienced chest pains and was rushed off to the hospital for an artery-clearing procedure called a *cardiac catheterization*.

It took two separate catheterization procedures to get the artery cleared. The first attempt at clearing the artery was a failure because the shape of my artery would not allow the instrument to pass through it. After the first attempt at clearing the artery, I felt worse from the procedure and the medications than from the heart attack. I experienced shortness of breath, fatigue, chest pain, and worry and panic. I had none of this for the two days I was experiencing the symptoms of a heart attack. My doctor advised a second try, and in the meantime, I should try to take it easy. It would take two weeks before the next opening at the hospital. However, there I was, swimming in worry, panic, and pain.

And then, I experienced a moment of synchronicity. At one point during my ordeal, I was in the emergency room at our local hospital. A friend of mine, Jerry Bass, was also there at the time for treatment of a sinus infection. As it turned out, his sinus infection was actually the symptom of a brain tumor, and he passed on a short time later. Jerry was a devotee of a spiritual teacher from India, and he had given me a jar of water that was blessed by his spiritual teacher. At age forty-four and under the stress of heart disease, I accepted the jar of water without hesitation.

I was sitting on my couch following my release from the hospital after the first attempt at unclogging my artery and decided to take a sip of the holy water. As soon as I took the water into my mouth, I heard, in my head, an angry voice of a woman. As strange as it sounds, under my current circumstances I listened with only a little trepidation. I did have some experience with listening to my inner voice, but this was different. She identified herself as my heart and was disturbed, to put it lightly. She said that I had neglected my heart. I was under too much stress at work and at home. I felt this was normal, being busy with the many things a young-middle-age man would be and with two children.

My heart would speak to me anytime I sat quietly relaxing, which I tried to do most of the time. The ranting and raving went on for at least two days. My doctor recommended that I undergo a stress test to see how much of my heart had been affected. I did not see why I should go through a stress test. I was under so much stress and was still alive. That should suffice. But no, a special stress test was needed, one in which I would be starved for about eighteen hours, and during that time a radioactive dye would be injected into my body.

The night before the stress test, I was lying in bed, miserable, when the voice came again, but this time the voice was compassionate. It said that I was okay, and it would guide me and support me through this. A great relief began to come over me. The next morning and afternoon, I took part in the stress test, and I felt wonderful on the treadmill. I felt that I was indeed supported and guided through this. The results, however, were discouraging, as one-eighth of my heart was damaged and another one-eighth of my heart was not receiving oxygen during exercise. My doctor recommended that I try the catheterization procedure again. There was a window of opportunity of about three weeks following a heart attack when it is still possible to open the artery.

The night before the second try at catheterization, I had a meditative experience that a finger was moving through my artery and opening it up. The next day at the hospital, while the doctor was doing the procedure, he stated that my artery was about 15 percent open, and without this opening, he would not have been able to complete the procedure. He was successfully able to unblock the artery and place a stent (a wire mesh tube) in the artery to help keep it open.

Six months later, I had another catheterization to check on the stent. It was a new type of stent, and the researchers behind the stent requested another look. The stent was fine, and the doctor said there was no sign of a heart attack. The one-eighth damage to my heart had been reversed. I truly believe that my treatment was done with a combination of traditional Western medicine and spiritual healing. I could not have healed without either one.

Currently, there is a separation between medical science and spiritual practice in our health care system, but this is softening. Medical science has its focus on the power of technological advances to treat our diseases. Indeed, the treatment and cure rate for heart disease, cancer, and some genetic disorders can be directly attributed to technological advances promoted by medical science. An example of scientific progress is the treatment of heart disease with angioplasty, stents, bypass surgery, transplants, medications, and valve replacements. And we, as patients, have benefited from many more. At the same time, there is a presence of prayer from clergy and patients and their families. Changes in lifestyle and diets have created an increase in good health and in disease prevention.

Our reliance on technology has increased, and at times, our attention to spiritual healing gets lost in the shuffle. As health care professionals, we are trained mainly on diagnosing disease and how to cure it. At the same time, many of us, as patients, do not take personal roles in the treatment of our diseases and the maintenance of our health.

Spiritual-energetic practice, including energetic healing, is concerned with treating the person and looking beyond the physical form and the physical manifestation of disease. It is my wish for people of medical science and practitioners of spiritual (energetic) healing to find a common ground. This foundation could create a working relationship between science and spiritual practice. Our efforts would promote the integration of medical science and energetic healing. This integration of our medical system with energetic healing would make it possible for a person to benefit from the latest medical technology, while receiving personalized care that would give meaning and purpose to his or her experience.

For over a hundred years, scientific research has been the basis of medicine and has led the way to the organization of our health care system. Insurance has been reluctant to include coverage of alternative care. In the late nineteenth and early twentieth century, medical practice in the United States transformed from methods based on data gained through observation and experience to scientific evidence-based systems. The natural healing modalities of homeopathy and herbology were lost or suppressed, even though, with their roots based in human experience, homeopathy and herbology have contributed to centuries of health care and maintenance.

The division resulted in a medical approach that emphasizes surgery and pharmaceutical medicine over other older forms of health care, to the point that our social and political systems support technological approaches exclusively. It is not only unpopular but professionally risky for practitioners to use alternative methods of healing. In the 1970s and 1980s, medical practitioners risked losing their licenses by offering nutritional therapies and homeopathy. Today that risk is still present, but it is diminishing due to popular acceptance of acupuncture, homeopathy, and nutrition. Some states in America have created licensing accreditation for acupuncturists and massage therapists.

Energetic healing modalities, such as homeopathy, nutritional supplementation, healing with prayer, the laying of hands, and herbal medicine, remain controversial. Dr. Marcia Angell, editor of the *New England Journal of Medicine*, has said that most consumers of alternative medicine "assume it's better because it feels better and is easier to understand." According to Angell, many members of the public seek the more attentive, individualized care of an alternative medicine practitioner; may be angry at the medical establishment; and don't understand science. "Some rely on alternative medicine alone, and that's the danger."[1]

Much work remains to create inroads into traditional medicine. I can foresee a time when alternative sources of healing are truly integrated into modern medical practice.

Promoting an understanding of how science and these energetic-based therapies can work together will encourage use of energetic healing. This will help our medical system to be open-minded and compassionate about complementary forms of healing. This is important, I believe, in creating health and healing institutions based on empathy and compassion, two fundamental elements of healing.

A large portion of the *Journey to Mudryi* focuses on bringing together the theories of science with the beliefs of spirituality. At the start of my journey, beginning with my childhood experiences with sickness and through my training in dentistry, I felt something was missing in my connection to myself and my patients. I had a desire to bring my scientific training and my experiences in spirituality together. This took much study and effort. I applied the information that I gleaned from these studies to maintaining health in my family life and then in treating patients. All along I assumed that I was alone in my pursuit. I was trained throughout my education to work alone and be independent. Then, after years on the journey, I discovered that human beings relate unconsciously, as well as consciously. This was most apparent during the teaching of co-cognition at the Foundation of Light. Participants, after a short focus and meditation, brought ideas and actions to their healing that could have happened only by synchronicity with the person being healed. I saw that this unconscious relationship, which I have termed *co-cognition*, was the missing link in my understanding of healing, and I found it could be made into a conscious relationship. Co-cognition opened up a new world of possibilities that illuminated many of the mysteries of healing.

At the end of my journey, the source of healing was waiting. Mudryi had always been there and had been my guide; I just had not seen it. The journey to Mudryi brought me out of the confusion of a paradox of why different methods of healing—such as homeopathy, acupuncture, and psychic healing—work in treating the same type of illness. It revealed to me the compassionate mind that had been missing in the healer/patient relationship. I dropped the assumption that one healing method is better than another. Left behind was the struggle to find the one right method, technique, or remedy. I let go of the need to get "better" before I could be a healer. I recognized that being a healer starts with acknowledging what I already had—a connection to the soul of the person receiving healing. This is all that I needed. I surrendered to the wisdom of Mudryi, the soul of the person in need of healing. This wisdom is the source of healing.

Listening to guidance from Mudryi, I let go of how things "have to be" and turned to a source of light that enriched my life, dissolved conflict, and brought clarity where there was confusion. Opening the disciplines of modern medicine to compassion would result in healers being open to the wisdom of the soul of their patients.

My journey to Mudryi began with a passion for something that was apparently unknowable and out of my reach. I traveled along paths that sometimes had clarity; other times I met dark roads that appeared to have no direction.

With gratitude, my journey brought me to a solid foundation. I reached a place where I have an integrated practice as a healer. I discovered that my work as a healer is guided by the source of healing, Mudryi. The purpose of this book is to recount my journey to Mudryi.

Many of the experiences and stories I will present may be seen as coincidental. Maybe the healings that occurred might have happened without my involvement in them. However, I believe in something called *synchronicity*. Jung defined synchronicity as an explanation of events that appear coincidental but that have a deeper meaning and connection. In my life a series of events and experiences led me on a journey. I do not believe the events and experiences are coincidental; rather, they all are meaningful and related stepping-stones.

I invite you to join me on this journey.

CHAPTER 1

AWAKENING TO THE
MYSTERIES OF HEALING

At any moment, what you know is what you will call life.
—Ira Kamp

Healing (literally, to make whole) is the
process of the restoration of health to an
unbalanced, diseased, or damaged organism.
When an organism suffers physical damage
or disease, *healing* involves the repair of living
tissue, organs, and the [psychological] and

biological system as a whole and resumption of normal functioning.[1]

A DEFINITION OF HEALING

Is healing the elimination of symptoms; that is, does the patient feel better? Does healing occur when the problem is cured and never returns? Does healing render a service so that the patient experiences a transformation? In my experience, a healing may not completely cure an illness. It can be a step on the way to becoming whole, and sometimes many steps on the journey to healing are needed to finally reach peace and balance. Healing can apply to any procedure that helps patients along their journey to health. Whether the healing completely relieves the condition or only brings comfort for a short time, in the context of this book, it will be considered a result indicating that healing has occurred. I must add that as long as it is done with an integrity in which the patient/practitioner relationship is honest, even if the patient is not aware (such as healing prayer), I will call this healing. I have a patient with chronic facial pain that I have seen for years in my office. The only relief that she gets is when she receives an injection of local anesthesia into the painful area. This procedure has to be repeated a few times a year, when the pain returns. She considers this a healing.

· · · · · · ●●●●●●●● · · · · · ·

I was sick many times as a child and always assumed that medicine held the magic to my healing. When I was fourteen years old, my older brother Steven and I were sitting at the kitchen table, having a conversation about medications. Steven made a comment that lit a light bulb over my head: "Taking aspirin didn't cure your illness; it only made you feel better." I did not yet understand that my body, given time, could heal itself and regain equilibrium. I had no knowledge that other things might come into play in healing, such as homeopathy, herbs, and a healing touch.

Steven's comment shifted my thinking, creating a desire to know how I had healed if it wasn't the result of the medicine. Since then, I have personally experienced two serious illnesses. Both times, in the midst of my suffering, the question arose, "How does my body heal?" I had a strong desire to find an answer.

· · · · · ● ● ● ● ◉ ● ● ● ● ● · · · ·

My ideas about traditional Western medicine came from my experiences as a patient and my studies in college and dental school. When I entered my traditional health care professional training in dental school, my perspective was only of traditional Western medicine. I believed myself to be a scientist, and I took on a scientific perspective of healing that served as my knowledge base as I entered my profession.

As I began my career in dentistry, I increasingly felt that something was missing in my approach to treating my patients. My search for this missing element led me to explore energy-based healing disciplines from both Eastern and Western traditions. I studied the methods of homeopathy, acupuncture, macrobiotics, nutrition, herbology, and craniosacral therapy, plus psychology and religious and spiritual healing. I experimented with these alternative treatments on my family and friends. Then, after seeing that the treatments made a difference, I brought some of these into my work in dentistry. I hoped that at least one of these approaches held the key to healing. But that was not the case.

SCIENCE TO ENERGY

Early in my journey, science held my imagination and my mind, my heart, and my soul. I was training in dentistry, probably the most physically based of the healing sciences, with engineering and construction principles guiding the treatment of patients. The physical basis for dental therapy did well in creating esthetic and functional reconstructions of diseased and injured teeth. However, the study of the psychology and well-being of the patients was rarely included in my training. Dental treatment appeared to me as a painful and difficult experience for patients, and I wondered if anything could be done to ease the harshness of their experience. Science was limited in its ability to answer my questions about healing. I began to look elsewhere.

In college, chemistry and biochemistry especially captivated me. Somewhere in the midst of memorizing organic chemistry reactions, it struck me that life could be one infinite and interconnected chemical reaction. I envisioned that this chemical reaction has been expanding since the beginning of time, like the ever-expanding universe, and becoming increasingly complex as it grows. I could see human beings, their bodies, and their behaviors (as well as animals, insects, plants, and all the other life-forms) evolving as part of an infinite chemical reaction. The reaction is analogous to branching rows of dominoes, lined up so that when the first domino is pushed, it falls into the second, which then knocks down the next one, and so on. However, traditional scientific theories did not satisfy my personal questions. Life could be an infinite chain of falling dominoes, with no apparent end to the game. I asked myself a question: "Who or what pushed the first domino?" Science had not been able to answer this question. Maybe some other realm, possibly philosophy, had an answer. I became philosophical in my explorations.

THE FROGS

In my senior year in college at the University of Buffalo, I was a research assistant in the biology laboratory of R. A. Flickinger.[2] We were studying DNA with the hope of finding a cure for cancer. My duty was to freeze frog eggs in liquid nitrogen and then centrifuge the frozen eggs to extract their DNA. I worked in the lab in the early hours while my fellow researchers were home, cozy in their beds, secure in the knowledge that I would complete the work they needed for their research by the time they awoke in the morning.

The solitude I experienced at 3:00 a.m. in the lab, while blizzard conditions often raged outside, started my wondering—from the unfairness of the menial part I was playing in the important scientific work of curing a disease to the question of what the meaning of my life would be in the future.

While worrying whether I would get any sleep before my 8:00 a.m. class, I wondered, *Why am I doing this?* The research felt as if it were part of some never-ending joke. Would frog eggs be processed in the same way from now until eternity? Were scientists trying to benefit society, or were they just after something to discover—any bit of information no one knew before—as part of a quest to be first at something? Were students doing the work to gain relevant experience or just to get credits to graduate? None of these questions thawed my frozen brain. Maybe my colleagues were dreaming of this while I contemplated that early morning in the lab, but they were more likely at peace in their sleep.

That night, everywhere I looked around this scientific lab, life appeared as a series of endless questions and labor. At 3 a.m., the meaning of our work faded away, and *out of my fatigue and struggle with frog eggs, arose a humorous and ironic idea: Although my colleagues and I are looking for an answer to cancer, my purpose is to find the truth that underlies all scientific endeavors.* Science could not answer my questions, so philosophy took over. I needed a purpose beyond the mashing of frog eggs. I was struck by the thought of humanity's search for an answer to the forever-flowing questions about life, including a cure for cancer and a purpose—a purpose that had a grand scheme behind it, created by a powerful and wise God. For me personally, that search was for the purpose of my own life and what, if anything, was guiding me. I truly felt that whether it was a conscious or an unconscious entity, some force had set life in motion. It had pushed the first domino.

· · · · · · ● · · · · · · · · ·

Science is defined as the systematic study of the structure and behavior of the physical and natural world through observation and experiment.[3] Science is a discipline that looks at the probability of phenomena and how one theory compares to other theories. I had questions that were never answered by science and maybe never will be. The questions I was asking—such as what was my purpose and what, if any, intelligence was guiding me—could not be satisfied through science but might be answered philosophically. I was inspired to look beyond science, into philosophical and spiritual ideas. Philosophy and spirituality held a potential to create a breakthrough in my consciousness, far beyond what science heretofore had offered me. This thinking took me beyond the physical and natural world. The frog eggs were a sacred offering, frogs sacrificing their lives for the good of humanity. And it was those frog eggs that led me to an awareness that

I saw science as a game I was playing. I was trained to follow the rules through a well-defined procedure to test a specific theory. My mind understood that I should play the game, but science could not answer life's big questions for me. Science would not show me the meaning or purpose of life for which I was looking. I needed something more. What I now see as my intuition brought questions and answers far beyond my experience in science.

My experience with the frog eggs was a turning point in my relationship with science, as well as a necessary step on my journey to Mudryi. Science did offer me an explanation about the physical world, but it did not satisfy my need for an explanation of how we heal using alternative modalities, such as acupuncture. Science left me without answers to the experience of death, mental and emotional disturbances, and spiritual matters, such as my purpose. Science became less important to me, although it was not eliminated from my life. I had to complete years of training that was based on scientific medicine before I became a dentist.

I had discovered that science could take me only so far in my desire to understand healing. I needed a perspective of wholeness—a joining of all perspectives into a unified view of life that gave equal meaning and purpose to science and to spirituality, one that bridged the two into a unified view.

Science is a powerful tool for unraveling the mysteries of the physical universe. Science is able to explain the form and energy phenomenon in the universe and gives explanations in terms of physics, chemistry, and biology.

Science serves us well in these areas. This does not mean that a scientific explanation for the questions I was asking is impossible, only that it hasn't yet appeared. For example, up to this time science has no conclusive explanation for what happens to our consciousness after death—it only describes how our bodies dissolve and recycle—but maybe someday the answer will come with scientific explanations.

THE BRIDGE

If I could not find my way to the answers I was looking for through the science in which I was involved, what path could I take? At this time the only philosophical basis that I had was through my religion and science fiction. These gave me only an intellectual experience of life, and my intellect had no answers. Reading what other people experienced and wrote about did not create an opening. I needed something to jump the gap in my knowledge about life, something to bridge the gap between my scientific thinking and maybe a spiritual life. My journey then took me in another direction.

> In my junior year in college I was introduced to meditation by a friend who had spent time with a teacher from India. As a twenty-year-old college student, I had never heard of meditation, and the mystery of Eastern philosophy attracted me. The attraction was not an intellectual one,

however. Something within was pulling me toward meditation. I went into it as a novice and read some books that spoke to surrendering my will to the teacher, how and what to eat, and how to meditate. Meditation, it said, would quiet my mind, giving me the experience of peace and well-being. It sounded interesting, and again it remained an intellectual experience for me.

My girlfriend asked me to join her meditation society, and, being open to new experiences, I agreed. I still had no idea what meditation was, but I wanted to know. Maybe this society would help.

I joined the meditation society via a long-distance induction ceremony. I was living in Buffalo, and the teacher in the society lived in Boston. When first we talked by telephone, he instructed me to sit in meditation at the same time he was meditating. The initiation would take an hour. I still did not know what this meant, but I expected to experience a rebirth, a flash of lightning that would lift me out of the unknown into a world of joy, happiness, and truth.

During that hour, I experienced one constant thought: *What am I doing here?* It was tedious and boring, and I was restless. If this was meditation—and especially an induction ceremony—I could not tell the difference between this experience and sitting in a boring religious ceremony. I did not have an ultimate experience and left the session bored and unsure about meditation.

I stuck with it; I cannot tell you the reason, other than I was dating the girl who introduced me to meditation. Over the next few months, my practice of meditation was difficult. Sitting for even five minutes made me excruciatingly restless. My mind fought to take over my consciousness every second, telling me to get up and do something. I was determined, and I kept on. After months of trying this, I gradually began to experience some unique sensations, such as my body physically shaking during the meditation time. I was told that this was energy moving through my body. The energy did not feel like I could control it and seemed to have a life of its own.

Energy—this was a new experience for me. I have energy in my body, and it makes me shake when I am sitting still and trying to be calm. The experience of energy in my body opened up a new possibility that my body was full of energy, and it had its own way.

At the same time, the United States was opening relations with China, and I heard about acupuncture. The United States had a diplomat in China who had appendicitis, and after his surgery, the Chinese doctors performed acupuncture on him. His recovery was fast and uneventful. The diplomat told this story, and the news spread about the wondrous results of acupuncture, telling how acupuncture could change the flow of energy in the human body to promote healing. *Was this the same energy that I was experiencing during meditation?*

This was an opportunity to see a connection—a bridge, so to speak—between my scientific mind, something I experienced as spiritual energy, and others who experienced healing energy using acupuncture. I was struck by the experience of the energy in my body during meditation. I could actually feel and observe my body as an energy field.

I felt that the energy used in acupuncture was the same energy that I experienced in meditation. I began to understand *chi*, as Chinese medicine calls it. Energy as the source of life became a possibility to me. Energy was the basis of life in all things—the movement of cells, biochemical reactions, my thoughts, the force behind the dominoes falling.

My courses in biochemistry frequently used the term *energy* in the explanation of life. So maybe the explanation I was looking for was that energy was the source of life. I walked on this bridge and carried these ideas and experiences with me through my dental training and into my practice of dentistry.

The One-Year Deal

My knowledge of Western medicine came from my experiences as a child who grew up with various illnesses and from doctor and dentist visits. If I was sick, doctors and medicines were the way to go. My experience of healing was to endure the disease, take medications to treat the disease, or have surgery to remove or correct whatever disease I had. The list included a hernia operation, tonsillectomy, wart removal, measles, mumps, chickenpox, colds, and flu. Any lessons learned came from understanding which medications to take, and these were usually prescribed by my doctor and given to me by my mother.

From my experiences with the many teachers involved in my training as a dentist, my perspective of healing remained taking medicine for illness and having surgery for diseases. In dental school, my training was based on how to perform surgery in a patient's mouth and what medications were best for supporting the surgery. There was a power in this. Doctors had the secrets to my health and would dole them out in the form of pills and surgery. This perspective on healing was all I knew. As I studied subjects in school like health, science blended into my knowledge and experiences like chocolate syrup blends into warm milk. Science was the foundation of all that I learned.

But after a time, I got tired of hot chocolate. I found medications worked much of the time, but my patients— and I—would experience side effects from the medications, such as nausea, loss of energy, digestive upsets, and pains not associated with the disease for which the medication was prescribed. As my practice of dentistry evolved, I increasingly felt that something was missing in Western medicine. I felt more and more uneasy in using only medications and surgery to treat disease. Well, what else could I offer?

· · · · · · ● · · · · · · · ·

WHAT IS APPLIED KINESIOLOGY (MUSCLE TESTING)?

I received treatment for back and neck pain, something common with dentists, from a local chiropractor who did something called *muscle testing*, or *applied kinesiology*, and prescribed vitamins for my condition.

Kinesiology, also known as biomechanics, is the study of body movement. Applied kinesiology (AK), which is also known as muscle testing, is a method of diagnosis and treatment based on the belief that various muscles are linked to particular organs and glands and that specific muscle weakness can signal [distant] internal problems, such as nerve damage, reduced blood supply, chemical imbalances, or other organ or gland problems. A manual muscle test in AK is conducted by having the practitioner apply a force to a specific muscle or muscle group, such as an extended arm or leg, while the patient resists. The response, which can be strong or weak, gives the practitioner information regarding the health or disease of the associated organ, gland or disease process. Practitioners assert that correcting this muscle weakness can help heal a patient's problem in the associated internal organ.[4] I found the results of muscle testing also had a correlation to finding where the energy of the patient was not in balance.

I spoke with my chiropractor about his treatments, and I became more curious about what he called "holistic healing." Holistic healing, he explained, is a diversified method of health care delivery. Done mostly by alternative practitioners, it takes into account the spiritual, mental, emotional, and physical parts of the patient. Practitioners of holistic health use nutritional and herbal supplements, body work (massage, Reiki, and yoga), and spiritual guidance to help their patients. He lent me a book, *Balancing Body Chemistry with Nutrition*[5] by Dr. Robert Peshek, a dentist, who used holistic care in his practice, including muscle testing and prescribing vitamins. The book contained scientifically sound articles and demonstrations of muscle testing. The work of my chiropractor and Dr. Peshek's writings intrigued me so much that I decided to give myself one year to study nutrition and other holistic health practices, such as homeopathy, acupuncture, and nutrition. I had no experience with any of these alternative modalities, and because of my scientific training, I was skeptical about whether they would work. Still, I was curious whether any of them had a valid basis. If after one year, none of these proved useful in my practice, I would stop exploring alternative approaches to healing and return to my current way of practice.

During the one-year period, I studied the methods of homeopathy, acupuncture, macrobiotics, nutrition, herbology, and craniosacral therapy, plus psychology and religious and spiritual healing. I took classes in nutrition, homeopathy, and herbology. I became certified in the use of acupuncture. All of these modalities claimed that the remedies and treatments would affect the energy of the patient positively and restore balance and health.

Holistic practice was considered heresy by the dental and medical professions, so to be safe, I first used homeopathy on my family and friends. I jumped at the chance to treat acute conditions such as rashes, fevers, painful limbs and backs, and mouth sores. Acupuncture and herbal remedies soon followed homeopathy. And then, after seeing that the treatments made a difference in their healing, I brought the new modalities to my work in dentistry. The first remedies used in my practice were homeopathic. I used homeopathic arnica, an extract made from a daisy like flower, for bruising and bleeding, after every extraction, because I was curious about their response to the remedy and hopeful that it would benefit them.

A Sweet Opportunity

I studied nutrition in the alternative literature, exploring topics such as caries, periodontal disease, ulcers, bacterial and viral infections, sinusitis, diabetes, heart disease, and cancer. At first I was impressed by the scientific presentation because the writings were worded very similarly to the pharmacology and physiology literature I had studied in dental school. However, I found there was little evidence of standard scientific research in the studies. Where did this information come from, if not from science? The authors sounded so assured that their information was accurate. By the time I realized there was very little science behind the alternative literature, I was already successfully using nutrition in my practice, and I felt there was no turning back.

In dental school, little attention was given to diet and its influence in disease. In fact, Coca-Cola was served at every function. It probably didn't help that Emory University was funded by Bob Woodruff, the president of the Coca-Cola Corporation in Atlanta, Georgia. In my residency and time in private practice, I heard of no other dentist or hygienist who mentioned nutrition counseling. So, it was a little out of the box for me to offer nutritional advice to my patients at that time. Today, such alternative nutritional guidance has become standard care.

I was in my trial year of using alternative therapies, including offering nutritional counseling in my practice. I observed that my patients benefited from changing their diets by eliminating refined carbohydrates and dairy foods and eating whole grains and vegetables. The reports I received from the patients were anecdotal but were influential nonetheless in my going forward with this work in alternative therapies. After receiving information about changing their diets, patients reported that their mouths felt healthier. These changes contributed to their improved oral health but also their general health. This kept me in the pursuit of something valid in nutrition and alternative healing.

· · · · · · ● ● ● ● ● ◉ ● ● ● ● ● · · · · ·

The alternative literature suggested that refined sugars affect not only our teeth but also the rest of our bodies in a negative way. I had attended a dental school where heavily sugared colas and coffee drinks were not discouraged and where no comments were made about sugar, other than its being one factor in the formation of dental caries.

I began recommending to my patients with cavities that they discontinue eating sugar. Then, something inside me said that if I was recommending avoiding sugar for my patients' better health, maybe I should take this advice myself. Although I didn't have cavities, I did eat a lot of sweetened foods. So, I chose to eliminate sugar from my diet. To my surprise, the migraine headaches I had been having since I was ten years old went away.

My need for scientific proof lost some of its significance. My chronic headaches—gone; my patients' health—improved. Nutrition clearly was an important part of health care.

THE SMALL THINGS

Later that year, I took a course in homeopathy taught by Robert Stewart, a homeopath based in Woodstock, New York, and New York City. In class, we were told that the remedies were diluted well below Avogadro's number (6×10^{-23}). This is the point at which a substance is diluted to where no physical substance remains. Robert said that the therapeutic quality was in the energy that was left after the original substance was removed through dilution. I sat there in confusion. The idea that something was therapeutic without having any physical substance in it was totally foreign to my thinking. My mind began considering the concept of energy, which is also called the *vital force* by some homeopaths.

The concepts behind homeopathy were intriguing, but what was inspiring to me were the benefits people were getting from the remedies.

As mentioned, I gave arnica, a homeopathic remedy for aiding the body to heal from trauma, to my patients after the surgical removal of their teeth. My patients did not understand how different this remedy was from allopathic medicine and had no idea what the effect would be on them. In one case, an older gentleman came back a week after having a tooth removed; I'd given him arnica following the extraction. The socket was healing, and he had no pain. Referring to the arnica, he asked, "What is this stuff? My jaw doesn't hurt, but my back, which always aches, doesn't hurt either!"

The standard theory of disease to which I previously subscribed is based on germs causing infections and on physical trauma causing injuries. So how could a remedy, with no physical substance in it, aid our bodies to heal? What was going on in the process of healing? Was it the placebo effect, as some scientific research indicated? The positive effects of homeopathy on the well-being of my family, friends, and eventually my patients opened up a possibility that homeopathic remedies—energetic in nature—somehow affected the human body. The remedies act through the body's energy. For example, an injury, such as the trauma following the removal of a tooth, causes an imbalance in our vital force (energy). Pain and swelling are the most likely outcomes. With the use of arnica after the removal of a tooth, the healing energy is enhanced, and the wound heals. In my experience, the injury resolves quicker and without the use of pain medications.

THE EASTERN WAY—THE GATEWAY TO ENERGY

An awakening happened after my training in acupuncture. During the course on homeopathy that Robert Stewart taught in Ithaca, he recommended that I meet Buzzy Tischler, a holistically oriented dentist in Woodstock. I visited Buzzy in 1983, and he suggested I get certified to use acupuncture in my dental practice. That summer I attended an intensive two-week acupuncture program. I discovered that the entire system of acupuncture was based on energy or chi (qi). Chi refers to the energy we use for the movement of our arms and legs; for our organs to perform their functions of breathing, pumping blood, and digesting food; and for our brains to think. Without chi, the body is a lifeless corpse. Chinese medicine provided a new paradigm, distinctly different from my Western medical training. It also described disease as an imbalance of energy (or chi) and promoted healing through the management of chi.

Studying the energy, or vital force, described in homeopathic literature and the organized system of traditional Chinese medicine gave me a context for thinking about the relationship between the physical and energetic changes that occur during illness and injury. Energy (chi) in the human body was described as an energy body, distinct yet intimately related to the physical body. It was the job of the acupuncturist or homeopath to assess the energy body and detect imbalances.

Walking home from work one day, I was contemplating how the energy body (chi) and the physical body (structure) are related. The answer came to me: "Energetic changes precede changes to our physical bodies." This meant that energy changes would precede the structural changes that occur during aging and sickness. Over time, imbalances in the energy, or chi, slowly manifest into the physical form. When energetic imbalances remain in the energy body for a considerable time, chronic illness—such as fatigue, digestive troubles, pain, and dysfunction in the physical body—can result. As a corollary, I postulated that structural changes can affect the energy body. For instance, if you get hit on the head, the physical changes affect the energy in your body; you become weak and lethargic.

One advantage of energetic assessment is that imbalances in the health of the patient can be detected earlier with energetic techniques, as compared to the physical tests of scientific medicine. Scientific medicine depends upon physical manifestations of disease before treatment is recommended. In acupuncture, accessing the pulse of a patient can determine the existence of disease before physical manifestations of the illness occur. Symptoms that indicate energy imbalances include fatigue, aches and pains, lack of mental clarity, anxiety, and other emotional disturbances. Scientific medicine has no explanation for these disease symptoms unless there is laboratory or radiographic evidence. Energetic healing assesses the energy body using techniques such as pulse diagnosis in acupuncture practice, applied kinesiology in chiropractic practice, or the repertorization* of symptoms in homeopathic practice. These diagnostic techniques allow healers using these and other energy-based modalities to treat people at much earlier stages of a condition.

A Puzzle

While studying energy-based healing during my training in the use of applied kinesiology (AK), I came across a puzzling pattern that threw conflict and confusion into my path. In the course, we were taught to use AK as a method of diagnosis. Its purpose was to evaluate the patient and find the most appropriate treatment.

AK is a technique in alternative medicine that claims to be able to diagnose illness or choose treatment by testing muscles for strength and weakness. AK is a form of biofeedback and is conducted by having the patient resist using a specific muscle or muscle group, while the practitioner applies a force. AK is not a treatment unto

---

* In homeopathy, the use of a list of a patient's symptoms that aid in the selection of an appropriate remedy

itself. It is only a method of diagnosis and evaluation of the most appropriate treatment for the condition of the patient.[6]

Different instructors presented contradictory directions for how to use AK as an assessment tool. Some teachers taught that strong-muscle resistance would indicate an appropriate evaluation of the condition of the patient. But other teachers taught that a weak-muscle resistance in the same muscle or muscle group used by the first instructor would indicate the appropriate evaluation of the condition on the same patient. Thus, either a strong reaction or a weak reaction could determine the condition of the patient. This seemed inconsistent, ambiguous, and paradoxical. In other words, it didn't matter which muscle was tested or how the patient reacted to the test. I witnessed that it only mattered what questions were asked about the patient and how the practitioner phrased the questions during muscle testing. No one else questioned this during my class. This gave me a preview of what was to happen on my journey.

In another example, two acupuncture instructors advocated needling people for varying amounts of time, depending on their conditions. One advocated a short time for tonification, which would stimulate the person's energy, and to needle for a longer time for sedation to calm the patient's energy. However, the other acupuncture instructors advocated leaving needles in for one hour, no matter what condition was treated. Based on their experiences, both instructors claimed their method led to successful treatments in their practices.

Much to my amazement, these apparent contradictions were sometimes presented at the same conference or even as part of the same course. No one else seemed alarmed by the paradoxes, but I wondered how one explanation of why a particular technique worked could be true if a different technique, with a different explanation for why it works, was just as effective. In contemplating this puzzle, I reflected on the following possibilities:

- One healer understands what he or she is doing and is accurate in his or her assessment and treatment, but the other is mistaken.
- Both healers are in error.
- Different and apparently contradictory techniques, although based on differing concepts, can be accurate in their assessments and effective in treatment.

I thought long and hard about these possibilities, and I chose to accept the third option: different explanations could be true, and many techniques can be effective in the treatment of disease. Although the following scenario did not happen, it is similar to something I heard in my classes. Following the testing of a patient with back pain and a digestive disorder, pain on eating, diarrhea, or constipation, a chiropractor using AK would report that there was a presence of a parasite. The chiropractor would recommend and perform manipulations for the back pain and prescribe herbs and dietary changes to treat the parasitic condition. An acupuncturist using

AK, however, found an energetic liver disorder in the same patient and recommended acupuncture to treat this condition. A dentist, after using AK, would report that an abscessed tooth was causing the condition and would recommend surgical procedures and homeopathic remedies for the same condition. All practitioners reported that their patients improved with their chosen therapies. I began to realize that the source of healing might not lie within the details of the method of healing but had another basis. There had to be some hidden wisdom that no one had yet recognized.

· · · · · · ● ● ● ● ● ● ● ● ● · · · · · · ·

First Healing Meditation: Becoming Aware of "What Is Present"

Start where you are. —Pema Chodron

The ability to focus will allow you to enter the other steps of mediation. A good first step is to become aware of *what is present for you*. In other words, what are you experiencing right now?

> ➤ Find a comfortable position. There will be no special posture at this point. You can be standing, lying, sitting, or walking.
> ➤ Be quiet. Open your awareness to *what is*. Make no judgment, and do not fix on any one idea or feeling.
> ➤ Notice your mind; listen to your thoughts. Let go of any reactions to your thoughts. Your mind will be only an observer.
> ➤ Notice your body. Feel the sensations arising within you.
> ➤ Notice what is around you. Again, just observe and feel without making up anything about *what is present for you*.
> ➤ Do this frequently throughout the day.
> ➤ This period of being with *what is present* can be as short as ten seconds. With practice, you can maintain this for longer and longer periods. Your objective is to attain this state of heightened awareness for at least a couple of minutes. The longer you can be with *what is present*, the easier you can access a meditative state.
> ➤ Don't worry about whether you are doing it the "right way," and don't rush yourself. You have a lifetime or more to learn how to meditate.

CHAPTER 2

SHIFTING PARADIGMS

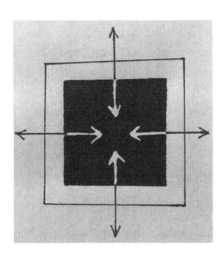

My first experience with using human energy occurred shortly after my acupuncture training. I attended an intensive acupuncture certification program led by Ralph Alan Dale. He was a music teacher who found the only effective treatment for his chronic dizziness was acupuncture. He was so inspired that he left his work as a music teacher and traveled to China to study acupuncture. He became one of the first licensed acupuncturists in New York State. During his training sessions, he spoke of the energy systems in the human body. The energy travels in channels, called *meridians*, in our bodies. Disease was seen as a block in the flow of the energy in the meridians. The blockage is the cause of the dysfunctional and painful conditions that accompany disease. The energy in the meridians can be manipulated through the use of needles to restore the normal flow. When Dr. Dale spoke, I visualized the blockage of energy as a river with a dam blocking the flow of water. Acupuncture treatment would remove the dam and allow the water (energy) to flow and restore health to the body.

Shortly after I finished my training, I used acupuncture to treat a neighbor who'd had foot pain for thirty years. The pain was in his left foot, a nagging pain that was not strong enough to prevent his walking but was an irritation for him. He could feel the pain when he rotated his foot. He pointed to an area inside his ankle. I placed two needles around the area of his pain, and in one treatment the pain went away and did not come back, for the year I was his neighbor. This was something I couldn't believe or explain to myself, for I was still skeptical of acupuncture at that time. My neighbor, however, knew it worked.

Before my training in homeopathy and acupuncture, I viewed energy as a force rooted in the physical universe. But now, energy in living things appeared to be more complex than a cascade of dominoes. The last domino had fallen, and there I was, wondering what else could explain healing. Science only studies those forms of energy it can measure and quantify. Physics defines energy by the function it performs and classifies it as potential, kinetic, or internal (nuclear). Chemistry classifies energy in terms of quantifiable bonds between atoms. Engineers work with thermal, electrical, and radiant energy. However, I did not see that science could show our emotions and thoughts as energy.

Not finding the answer in my scientific experience, I decided to check out an idea related to energy—to see if our ability to be self-expressive, our capacity to experience joy and tolerate pain, and the mental ability to think and to problem solve could arise from energy in our bodies. The question was, "Can a comprehensive explanation of energy be found that links all the various forms of energy, including scientific and nonscientific theories?"

· · · · · · ● ● ● ● ● ● ● ● ● · · · · · ·

THE PLACES WHERE SCIENTIFIC ANGELS FEAR TO TREAD

It felt like my scientific training held me in a place where anything not explained by science was not considered a certainty until scientifically proven. I felt that it was forbidden to go to places where my experiences could not be explained through science, places where scientists feared to tread.

Something needed to shift in my thinking. My experience with meditation showed me that life was more than a cascade of dominoes. Before, I saw life as a string of events, with cause and effect directing it. Now, with meditation, a new world of feeling peaceful and the experience of energy in healing was opening. I needed a new way to explain the complexities of the living world and to answer questions such as, "Who or what is the impetus behind the falling dominoes?" and "Why did I shake so much during meditation?"

The answer soon came in the study and discipline of energetic healing. I knew energy was an important element in the mysterious equation, so delving into the study of energy became my next focus.

· · · · · · ● ● ● ● ● ● ● ● ● ● · · · · ·

THE MEETING PLACE:
THE STRUCTURE OF ENERGY

An electric current (a flow of electric charge) has an associated magnetic field, regardless of the material (or space) in which the flow occurs. This is a *fundamental* part of electromagnetism, rooted in observation and quantified in law. I wish to emphasize that this phenomenon is considered fundamental in nature, which means there cannot be a "more" fundamental explanation (if there were, electromagnetism would not be fundamental).[1]

I refocused my thoughts on healing to a process with energy as the basis for healing. I was introduced to the concepts of electromagnetic fields, or energy that surrounds all living beings. Electrical currents in our bodies have been acknowledged for years through the use of electrocardiograms (EKG) and electroencephalograms

(EEG). The units of measurement used in these tests are millivolts (mv) and Hertz (hz). Brain waves and electrical conductivity in the heart have been found to vary with our degree of consciousness (awake or asleep) and the degree of health versus disease in the heart.

How does this apply to healing energy? I had heard of the energetic field around a person called an *aura*. Ampere's findings[°] give credibility to what some call auras.

> The aura is an electromagnetic field of energy that extends all around our body for about 4–5 feet (in an average healthy body) and appears to be depleted in cases of unhealthy persons. The aura of a person is directly connected to the level of health of the person. A person is considered to be Healthy in terms of Physical vitality, mental clarity, emotional well-being as well as highly positive spiritual energies. So, a person who is healthy at all these levels has a bigger and brighter aura and vice versa in the case of an unhealthy person.[2]

I had read and heard healers refer to *chakras*, or energy centers, in the human body. They can be seen as small auras emanating from the body. There are seven wheels of energy in the human body where the energy flows through. They start from the base of the spine through

---

[°] André-Marie Ampère (1775–1836), French mathematician and physicist, considered the father of electrodynamics

the crown of the head. To visualize a chakra in the body, imagine a swirling wheel of energy where matter and consciousness meet. This invisible energy, called *prana*, is a vital life force that keeps us vibrant, healthy, and alive.[3]

I could see that the electrical currents that the human body generates, such as the EKG or even the acupuncture meridians, produced an electromagnetic field. I looked at the practices of alternative healing, specifically acupuncture and hands-on healing. Both use the electromagnetic fields of the human body in their assessment and treatment of diseases, and now their practice made more sense to me. Acupuncture uses the energy in the meridians to assess and treat disease. Hands-on healing uses the perception of an aura through the healer's hands to assess and treat the patient.

In a paradigm based on energy, the *science* of electromagnetic fields and the practice of healing with energy are bridged. From an energetic healing point of view, electromagnetic fields validate the presence of the vital force that homeopaths work with, the chi of acupuncture, and the prana described in the practice of Ayurveda yoga. Now I could create a possibility of relating the findings of an EKG to the quality of the human aura.

Richard Gerber eloquently describes the electromagnetic field in all living things. In *Vibrational Medicine*, he depicts the electromagnetic field as a template of energy that emanates from and surrounds an organism. This field is similar to the infrared energy that radiates from all living things. Gerber portrays electromagnetic energy as a holographic representation of the organism. In one remarkable example that Gerber cites,[4] known as the "Phantom Leaf Effect," the energy field surrounding a leaf maintains the shape of the original leaf, even if part of the leaf is cut off.

The existence of an electromagnetic field encompassing all living things has been confirmed and documented by scientists such as Harold Burr [5]and Semyon Kirlian[6] and is today acknowledged as a scientific reality. While no well-developed scientific theory of the function and purpose of the electromagnetic fields that surround organisms has yet emerged, much has been written on the subject. The disciplines of acupuncture, craniosacral therapy, therapeutic touch, and Reiki therapy all refer to electromagnetic fields in their explanations of how these systems work.

A Model of Energy

During my acupuncture training, I was taught that energy flows through the body in a series of circular paths, with each path or meridian starting in one place, flowing through the various regions of the body, and then returning to the same place it started. This cycle repeats as long as we are alive. The flow of energy throughout the body is analogous to the flow of blood. After blood is pumped from the heart, it flows through every part of the body before returning to the heart to be cycled again.

As I envisioned previously, the energy flows within these paths like the current in a river. In acupuncture, disease is seen as a block in the flow of energy. I saw this blockage as a dam in the river. On one side, the water (energy) pushes against the dam. The energy is strong but stagnant. On the other side of the dam, the flow is just a trickle; the energy there is weak. Acupuncture seeks to release the dam so that the energy flows again, restoring health. My neighbor's painful foot, in Western medicine, likely would have been diagnosed as chronic arthritis. In energetic healing, it is seen as a blockage in the movement of energy. It could have been caused by an injury that never fully healed. The pain had been present for three decades, but when the dam was broken up and the energy flow returned, his pain vanished.

A PERSONAL TOUCH

Opening my viewpoint of healing to include the existence of an energy field brought other new techniques into my practice. A chiropractor, Dr. Alan Sachs, who I met in my acupuncture training, imparted further insights into Applied Kinesiology (AK). He showed me the importance of touching the patient's body during the assessment of their health. He explained like acupuncture, AK is based on an energetic theory of healing. Touching the patient gave him a connection into their energy field. He revealed that is not the reaction of the muscles that is essential, but rather, what is most significant is the condition of the underlying energy in the body. I later attended a class presented by the originator of AK, Dr. George Goodheart, and began using AK in my practice. So began my journey through the use of applied kinesiology to evaluate the human energy field.

My scientific mind still kept me in a place of skepticism about energy healing. I made a commitment to examine the results of all my endeavors in energetic healing, with the goal of finding common and predicable outcomes of the therapies. Then I ran across a book that changed some of my skepticism. Fritjof Capra's book *The Tao of Physics* created a new paradigm for me.[7]

According to Capra, energy and life are not as simple as we once thought. Chemical reactions cannot always be predicted. It is as if chemical energy—and thus biochemistry and life itself—has a mind of its own.

The following story illustrates life's unpredictability.

· · · · · ● ● ● ● ● ● ● ● ● · · · · ·

Tom was a high school student interested in a career in dentistry who came to observe our dental practice for a few hours. He arrived shortly after we had started our day. I was in a treatment room, and he was watching and listening from the hallway outside. My patient was complaining of pain in her temporomandibular joint (TMJ), and I was using applied kinesiology—or muscle testing, as some describe the procedure—to evaluate her condition.

Tom observed the process and then asked me about the work I was doing. I was excited that a student would be interested in the alternative approach I was using. I described the idea of muscle testing and some of the principles behind the work. When I asked Tom if he would like to experience muscle testing, he readily agreed.

The muscle test procedure that I use is called the "O ring" test. It tests the reaction and strength of the muscles between the forefinger and thumb when the patient holds them together in a ring shape. First, the practitioner applies just enough pressure so that the fingers do not separate but would with a little more pressure. Some people are strong and some are weak, so the practitioner must adjust accordingly. No more or no less pressure is used from then on.

Once a pressure level is established, the next step is to challenge the patient. A challenge is accomplished by producing a stress to the body of the patient. It could be touching the skin at a specific acupuncture point or chakra, verbalizing words that could stress the patient, or moving my hand against the natural flow of an acupuncture meridian.

My patient's pain in her TMJ was on the left side. I was testing for the source of the pain. TMJ pain and dysfunction can be caused by repeatedly clenching the teeth (called *bruxism*), trauma to the joint and surrounding muscles, or a blockage of the energy of the acupuncture meridians running through the area. It could be one of these or a combination. The muscle testing revealed that the patient did not have dysfunction in the joint; rather, the pain was from a blockage in the energy. She was treated with acupuncture, nutritional supplements that improved the flow of energy, and changes in her diet, including eliminating coffee and refined foods. Her symptoms discontinued soon after.

When I left the treatment area, Tom asked me about the procedure he'd witnessed. I explained the testing by demonstrating applied kinesiology on him. (We were talking in a narrow hallway.) Tom was very tall (about six foot three, which is my height) and a strong, athletic type. He was able to put up a lot of resistance, but I found the right amount of pressure to separate his O ring. As a challenge for Tom, I moved my hand against the normal flow of an acupuncture meridian (called the *conception vessel*) that runs up the midline of the body to the face. Holding my hand an inch or two away from his fully dressed body, I moved my hand in a downward motion. I repeated the movement three times.

By convention, the practitioner has three seconds after the challenge to test the O ring.

When I applied pressure to Tom's fingers, they separated—the normal response I expected to happen. What happened next, however, was unexpected. Tom rolled his eyes back and up, an expression that I initially took as one of disbelief, but rolling his eyes was just the beginning. Next, Tom's whole body rolled backward, and he slid down the wall to the floor. My mind did not initially comprehend what was happening. Then I realized that this strong athletic boy had fainted! After a few minutes of first aid, Tom regained consciousness.

The question going through my mind was, *How could this procedure have produced such a significant reaction?* After all, this was like tickling somebody with a feather, not hitting him over his head with a hammer.

· · · · · · ●●●●●●●●●●● · · · · ·

There may be two explanations of why Tom fainted.

> ➢ He was very tired and probably dehydrated from being out in the sun for a long time the day before. It could have been coincidental that Tom fainted at that time.
> ➢ I did not know his history of the day before at the time he fainted. After regaining consciousness, Tom told me that he was fatigued. It is likely that

being tired made him more susceptible to the slight challenge to his body.

Looking back, I feel that Tom's reaction was an unpredictable opportunity for me. I witnessed an effect of the energetic challenges to the human body, and this time they had a profound result.

The challenge to Tom's electromagnetic field with applied kinesiology and its result altered my skepticism. Even though there were some other influences present at the time that likely contributed to weakening Tom's health, I know the effect of the energetic challenge was not an illusion; it was real. Tom became unconscious after I waved my hand in front of his body. My intention was to demonstrate energetic testing, but the challenge to Tom's energetic field resulted in Tom's going from a conscious state to an unconscious state, right then and there. This experience confirmed for me that the energy field is real and that the effects of its use can be profound. The power of the result of this energetic challenge to Tom inspired me to go forward and learn more.

· · · · · · ● ● ● ● ● ● ● · · · · ·

Healing Meditation 2

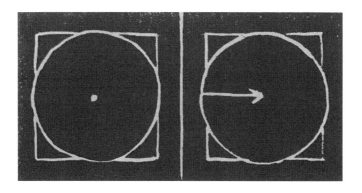

Focusing

Meditation is the prolonged focusing of the attention in any direction and the steady holding of the mind on any desired idea.

The secret of getting ahead is getting started.
—Agatha Christie[8]

Perhaps the greatest boundary we set for ourselves is the one between the conscious and less conscious parts of our own minds. We all need a way to gain deeper understanding of what goes on inside our minds when we are awake, asleep, or just not paying attention. Meditation is one way to pay attention long enough to find out.

Focusing is something that we already do in our lives, allowing us to concentrate on what is in front of us—but the depth of this focus remains superficial.

The events around us in the world can rob us of our

attention, and our concentration is gone. The mind that wanders is the source of all types of suffering. Focusing brings us back, and with prolonged focus, calm and peace arise.

By prolonging our focus on what is, our minds slow and may even come to a standstill. We can unlock the potential and unused ability that lies within a consciousness that is peaceful and calm. This is called *meditation*.

We maintain a balance of mindfulness and happiness for ourselves, bringing contentment and direction to life in a way not possible through any other technique. Healers perform their energetic healing within the quiet, peaceful mind. We will call this the compassionate mind. The compassionate mind is consciousness in which we can share the suffering of others. In this state, however, we, as healers, do not suffer.

In Healing Meditation 1, we practiced being aware of what is present for us and focusing on it for short periods. Healing Meditation 2 involves lengthening our practice to at least five minutes and has a goal of ten minutes.

With prolonged focus, we can create a long period of quiet and compassion. The attribute of being present with someone else's suffering, with tolerance and kindness, can become a possibility.

> ➤ Again, start where you are. There is no special posture at this point. However, if you want to sit quietly, it is okay. Notice your mind, listen to your thoughts, and feel the sensations arising within you. Make no judgment, and do not fix on any one idea.

This can be accomplished standing, lying, sitting, or walking.

➤ Also, gently stretching your body before or even during the prolonged focus can help.

➤ Be with what is present until the distractions of your own pain, tiredness, excitement, or thoughts recede. You can begin with two-minute periods and work up to ten minutes.

➤ When a calmness is reached, there now will be a possibility for heeding the wisdom of the present moment.

A Taoist Meditation Prayer

Close your eyes, and you will see clearly.

Cease to listen, and you will hear truth.

Be silent, and your heart will sing.

Seek no contacts, and you will find union.

Be still, and you will move forward on the tide of spirit.

Be gentle, and you will need no strength.

Be patient, and you will achieve all things.

Be humble, and you will remain entire.[9]

CHAPTER 2

BIOENERGY

*We tend to discount traditional medicine or alternative
medicine until we get sick. Then—and only then—
do we consider crossing the bridge.*

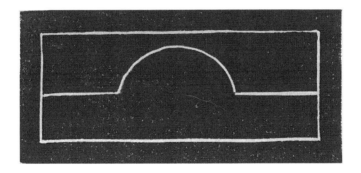

I was in a seminar for personal growth and development
with about fifty people. The participant sitting next to me
was constantly coughing. When I asked if he was okay,
he said yes but that he had been experiencing a cough for
about three months without resolution. The week before,
I had taken a class on energetic healing, where human
bodies are considered equal parts of energy and matter;
our attention was on the energy.

My healing class taught me that healing starts by mentally creating a desire to heal. A very short period of focus or meditation is necessary. Out of this intention, the next step is to think about the person in need of help and to be with that person in a quiet calmness. Then, visualize a method of healing. The method could be something with which you already have experience or an improvisation. In my class I was taught "hands-on healing"—using my hands to heal. In this method, the process begins with laying one or two hands on the patient. I learned about the feeling of the human energetic field. With a little experience, I was able to feel a "pressure," such as when two magnets with the same polarity are brought into contact with one another. I could interact with the field by visualizing, and I could feel energy leaving my hand or being absorbed by my hand. I could change the direction of energy flow by moving my hand—bringing my hand closer or farther away, depending on what felt right to me. The changes in temperature that my hand felt were also considered important indicators of what was needed. The energy field could feel weak or strong or warm or cold, depending on the condition of the patient.

I did not tell my neighbor of my intention to help him. After a short period of attention, I envisioned that his body was energy. With this in mind, I placed my right hand at the center of his back (at the level of his lungs) without touching his back—my hand was about an inch away. I had learned that contact with the patient was not necessary.

I could feel my neighbor's energy field; it was cold and weak. I focused on allowing energy to flow from my hand into his lungs. I was aware of a magnetic type of feeling, as if opposite poles of a magnet were being brought together. My hand vibrated; I felt alternating coolness and heat. I remained with him for about ten minutes. I do not think he was aware of my process to help him; as mentioned, my hand was not in physical contact with his back. He said nothing to me.

His cough stopped after about a minute or two, but I got a feeling that I should continue holding this area for the full ten minutes. After I did, I gently removed my hand from his back and said nothing to him.

It's interesting that he had no idea of what was happening, and I did not tell him of my intention, which brings up the point of getting a consent from our patients before we perform healing on them. My feeling is that sometimes it is important to tell our patients about the process, especially if we physically touch them. In terms of prayer and healing from a distance, however, I feel the need for consent is not always necessary. How often is prayer sent to an ill patient without his or her knowledge or consent?

· · · · · · ●●●●●●●●●● · · · · ·

The Dawn of Energy

The journey to Mudryi progressed into my searching for explanations of energy fields. My investigation led me to what Gerber and others called the energy field surrounding an organism—*etheric matter*. Practitioners of energetic healing have conceptualized the energy field of the human being as the etheric body. The etheric body is composed of energy that vibrates at a higher frequency than the matter that composes the physical body, but it is still made of the same matter/energy as the physical body. Gerber compares the relationship of the physical body and the etheric body to that between water and steam. The inherent character of both is the same; it is the vibratory state of the atoms and molecules that varies.

The etheric body is not limited to individual organisms. There is actually some compelling scientific evidence that shows that when human beings resonate emotionally in response to an event, the power of their collective resonant emotions is increased exponentially and either creates coherence or discoherence in the field.[1] From my classes at the Foundation of Light, taught by Kate Payne and Mabel Beggs, I learned that an energy field also arises from communities, the earth, the solar system, and the universe. Their information was taken from the esoteric writings of Alice Bailey; David Tansley, DC; and Helena Petrovna Blavatsky. It has been proposed that by understanding the structure and function of the energy field of a seed, a bird, or a human being, we can begin to understand the energy field of the universe. This idea of the small (microcosmic) representing the large (macrocosmic) is a fundamental principle of energetic healing. Everything in the universe is connected through a ubiquitous energy field and this connection opens up the possibility of a bridge between science and energy and, quite possibly, also to spirit.

The idea of an energetic field surrounding the physical form was postulated by Dr. Samuel Hahnemann in the early nineteenth century. He is best known for creating a system of alternative medicine called *homeopathy*.

> Patricia arrived in my office with a very bad toothache. Using dental diagnostic tests to evaluate the vitality of her tooth, I determined that her tooth was not vital and I could see from an x-ray that she had an abscessed tooth.
>
> Before she left, I felt that I could find something to help with muscle testing. Part of my equipment that helps determine the energetic cause and treatment for disease was a series of vials that contain diluted preparations of medications. The vials were manufactured with the concept of homeopathy, where the substance itself has an energy field, and this field can interact with the energy of the patient. Homeopathy can be used to heal patients with acute or chronic conditions. Homeopathic remedies also can be used, just like medications, to relieve pain in acute situations, such as a painful tooth. In homeopathy, the more a substance is diluted, the more potent the energy of the substance becomes.

These particular vials were diluted in ethanol to 1/30,000 of the original full-strength antibiotic. The energy can have varying degrees of benefit to the patient. The vials are made of glass so the energy of the substance within the vial can pass through the glass. I used the O ring test, strengthened when vials of antibiotics touched her. One particular vial of erythromycin tested as particularly effective. When the vial of erythromycin was placed in Patricia's hand, she reported that her pain immediately stopped. She did not know what was in the vial. When I removed the vial from her hand, the pain returned. As long as the vial was in contact with her, there was no pain. I deduced that the energy field of this particular substance had a profound effect on her energy. Although it would not cure her abscess, the fact that her pain immediately ceased was spectacular.

She insisted I leave the vial with her. At this point I explained to her that she needed root-canal therapy or to have the tooth removed. She wanted nothing to do with losing a tooth and chose root-canal treatment. I phoned our local root-canal specialist, and he said that he could see her right away.

I placed the vial in her pocket so she would remain pain-free, and she left for continued care with the root-canal specialist.

· · · · · ●●●●●●●●●●● · · · · ·

The etheric body is the point of access for the energetic healer and creates a template for energetic healing work. Acupuncture works through the stimulation of the energy or chi. Homeopathy affects what is called our *vital force*. Chakra therapy uses the energy centers located along the front and back of our bodies. Some energetic healers use the chakras as their source of access to the energetic field and treating energy imbalances. All of these and more therapies prescribe the use of the etheric body. Medical science has acknowledged energy in the physical form. Standard medical practice does test the energy produced in the body, such as the electrical energy patterns of the heart shown by an EKG or the electrical energy patterns in the brain shown by an EEG. Practitioners of energetic healing view this electrical energy as part of the entire human energy field.

Humans are beings of energy, and the quality and quantity of energy can be perceived in our thoughts and actions and when we speak. I have observed that when a patient is restless, in pain, or troubled, he or she speaks in an agitated manner. When patients are tired and in pain, they speak in a weak and fragile manner. I could now relate that how patients express their concerns and what they are feeling are expressions of the state of their energy.

When I am practicing dentistry, one of the first questions I ask my patients is, "How are you feeling? What hurts?" This is part of a bedside manner that is a friendly way of gaining information. I can gain insights into the general vitality of the patient, as well as his or her specific source of oral pain. Practitioners of energetic healing also ask these questions, and they use the patient's response as an evaluation of their energy. In a sense, practitioners of traditional and alternative health care assess the energy of their patients.

I began to see that all substances, including the allopathic medications that I was prescribing, contained energy. As in Patricia's case, I could test for the best medication, such as a specific antibiotic, with applied kinesiology.

I was not alone in this work. I found support from other health care practitioners in Western medicine who were using energetic methods in their practices. One physician, an oncologist, acknowledged the presence of energy in the medications he was using. He worked with what he called *bioenergetic testing* (BET) to find the optimal chemotherapy medication for his cancer patients. He used a computerized diagnostic instrument that measured skin resistance. He said that skin resistance varied with exposure to environmental stress, and the skin reacted to these stressors by changing the amount of moisture it contained. The medications were considered to be able to energetically stress the patient and these reactions could be measured electronically. He and his work were inspiring and supporting for me on my journey.

I also found support from many chiropractors interested in energetic healing. They were trained in traditional chiropractic care and now were branching out into applied kinesiology. Some of my colleagues in dentistry were using BET to determine the tolerance and effectiveness of dental materials for their patients. Truly, it felt like my journey was moving forward with increased momentum, generated from the work and camaraderie of other practitioners.

A New Language

I continued my relationship with science and created ideas at every opportunity that would blend and unite science and energy in my life and in my dental practice. Homeopathy, acupuncture, applied kinesiology, and nutrition were integrated into my practice. I gave patients a choice of therapies to use with allopathic medicines. Arnica, a standard homeopathic remedy, was given routinely to my patients following traumatic treatments, such as extractions. Following the extraction of a tooth, the patients would report that there was no need for the pain medication because the homeopathic remedy helped.

Science and Scientific Language

Through language we share information. Our minds are able to integrate this information and create a knowledge base from which we make our choices. In this light, there is the possibility that our evolution depends upon the language used in conversations.

In the conversations that I had with people outside of the scientific world (dental supply companies; sellers of nutritional supplements and natural remedies), I noticed something disturbing: scientific language was used even though there was no scientific basis behind what was said. Alternative healers were not immune to this either.

It appeared to me that alternative healers used scientific language to describe their theories and work. They must have some trust in the scientific method; otherwise, they would not be speaking that way. And after listening carefully to what was said, I concluded that their information had little or no scientific support. It struck me that scientific language was used to bring credibility to their subject!

Since then, I have concluded that the use of scientific language in our culture is ubiquitous, and the use of unqualified scientific language is endemic. Could it be that our social interactions, advertisements, and business interactions are fraught with scientific language that is not based on scientific studies? In my experience, the answer is yes, which leads me to believe that either we are not aware, or we do not care what words we use when speaking. To bring integrity to our work, we must be aware of how we use our language in our work.

· · · · · · · ● · ● · · · · · · · · ·

My quest led me to take many courses and seminars in alternative healing, including acupuncture, homeopathy, homotoxicology, polarity therapy, Gestalt therapy, herbal medicine, and many others. Without exception, all the facilitators spoke using science-based language. Scientific language initially arises out of the scientific process. Many of us who practice energetic healing use scientific language. Whether we are aware of it or not, we use scientific language to create an atmosphere of credibility around our work.

For example, in Chinese medicine, the meridians are named after the organs of the body, such as liver, lung, heart, and spleen. These words, although they do not have the same meaning in Chinese, appear to give more credibility to the work. Terms not readily associated with science, such as triple heater (an acupuncture meridian) or chi take some understanding before they are accepted.

In a course on alternative biological medicine, I witnessed practitioners using computer technology to test patients and to find a diagnosis for the patients' illnesses. The results included parasites, nutritional deficiencies, and toxins. However, when testing the same patient, various practitioners did not get the same diagnosis. This caused some confusion in my understanding of biological medicine. Repeatability of results by other researchers under the identical controlled conditions is a cornerstone of science and, by extension, conventional medicine. What was taught did not arise out of conventional medicine. Out of this muddle, I became aware of a new milestone: In the use of any alternative bioenergetic diagnostic method, the findings are not consistent from practitioner to practitioner.

Up to this point, science was the truth. It is baffling that an idea expressed in scientific language could be heard and accepted, even though there was no scientific basis to the statement. I had to remind myself that the validity of scientific knowledge does not solely depend on language. It depends on having the scientific research to back it up.

I could find no scientific research supporting the use of this specific computer program as a tool for the diagnosis and treatment of diseases. In this case, the computerization of information created what appeared to be a scientific basis for their results, giving the results an apparent credibility.

I came to accept this way of exchanging ideas as normal behavior in the alternative healing community. Scientific language is used by alternative healers to bring credibility to their communication and their work.

Consider these two statements:

- The use of an electronic instrument, the EKG (electrocardiogram), can determine the state of the health of your heart.
- The use of an electronic instrument, the EAV (electroacupuncture according to Voll), can determine the state of the health of your heart.

Both statements use scientific language. Both methods of evaluating the heart claim to produce data that can be used to determine the health of the heart. However, statement 1 is based on valid scientific research, whereas the second statement is not.

The careless or unconscious use of scientific language has caused people who value science as the best way to determine truth, to mistrust energetic healing methods. The ensuing confusion has resulted in a polarized stand on the validity of energetic healing in the medical community. This has been one of the reasons why science and spirit have remained separate.

I was left with no center, no balance on the source of healing. At one time, I had faith that medical scientists had exclusive knowledge, that their science held the certainty in the process of healing. However, I found that scientists restricted the reasons for healing to a set of their own standards and ideals and rejected any healing modality that did not have scientific validation. Any idea out of the scientific box is dismissed until it is examined under an experimental setting and proved to be effective.

On the other hand, energetic healing was a mish-mash of ideas with no unifying principles that could lead to understanding and predictability. Practitioners use of scientific language was not helpful in getting to the source of healing.

At the course I attended, the diagnostic instrument consisted of a computer with a probe that could sense electrical conductivity of the patient's skin. I considered that it was not the computer that produced the results but rather that these practitioners were using their personal insights through the computer to create the data. When I used the diagnostic computer, I found that the diagnostic information depended upon the quantity of pressure that I placed on the patient, rather than the computer knowing the right answer. The variation of pressure could be attributed to the personal insight of the practitioner, what I later discovered is *dowsing*, rather than the patient's response and the computer's analysis of the testing.

The challenge for me was to bring these two approaches together: science and personal insight. This insight I would come to know later as intuition.

THE COMMON DENOMINATOR

My experiences led me to the premise that energy is the common denominator in life. At first, I thought the source of healing was understanding how this energy is organized in the human being. This turned out to be only part of the mystery. Energy was the ubiquitous element in life that brought science and spiritual healing into a unified paradigm. But now energy did not give me enough of an explanation. The concepts of energy brought me to the doorstep of another level of understanding. What lay behind the door was something I had yet to discover. I had come from a place anchored in science and had journeyed to a land where energy held the mystery of our healing. And then my trek took me to a new ground, one that is rooted in a more spiritual perspective. I could feel its potential as a rich resource of wisdom that all human beings could know and from which they could benefit.

Concurrently, my practice of meditation continued in the realm of energetics. The concept of a human energy field gave birth to an appreciation of my human consciousness in meditation. While in meditation, I experienced feelings that were apparently different from the sensations of my physical body—sensations such as lightness, peace, pulsations throughout my body distinct from heartbeats and breathing were common. Being in meditation brought my mind into a state of peace and balance. I found that meditation could increase my tolerance for illness and promote healing. If I was sick with the flu or had physical pain, meditation could help ease the pain. By focusing on a peaceful way of being, the discomforts of illness would dissolve. Meditation was a big influence in my recovery from my heart attack.

My awareness of energy clarified what I felt during meditation. I also noticed that acupuncture stimulation of my energetic field produced the same sensations as when I was meditating. In fact, the chi in acupuncture, the vital force in homeopathy, and the rhythms found in craniosacral therapy felt as if they originated from the same phenomenon. I felt that there was a common source to all the energies that were described by the various disciplines.

I saw the common denominator in the etheric body. It was a reservoir of energy and could connect with all the energy available in the universe. I experienced the ability of energy to leave my etheric body and join another body or be absorbed from other beings into my own. I experienced the energy exchange with a person sitting next to me with the uncontrolled cough. I felt this energetic connection through the energetic healing I personally experienced when I was receiving care from a dentist, physician, physical therapist, chiropractor, or massage therapist.

The etheric body, although integrated with the physical body, can be conceptually separated from the physical body. Gerber writes that the etheric body has encoded information about the organization of the physical body. In reality, it is the organizing principle of the etheric body that maintains and sustains the human body. The energies of the etheric body have qualities that move the physical systems toward states of higher organization. In disease, the etheric body loses its power. Dissipation of the etheric energy eventually leads to death. The influence of the etheric energy of healers allows the body of the patient to reorganize toward health.[2] But the energy exchange is not a one-way street. Energy from the patient also influences the energy of the healer. I have experienced that during the interaction of my etheric body with my patient's energy. I gather information that is felt and interpreted by my body and mind.

I could visualize my body and the body of my patients as a form in light, in the shape of the physical body. The etheric bodies of my patients, through which I could now connect and share experiences beyond our physical nature, opened a new pathway on my journey. Human energy fields were a template, a hologram in the form of light, where the healer and patient could exchange energy and even communicate, in a subtle way, with each other. The energy exchanged between our etheric bodies could create balance—in the patient as well as in me, as I would later find out.

Energy served as the foundation of my healing work and could be used to describe all physical and energetic healing methods. The subtle communications that I received challenged me, inspired me, and guided me on the next steps on my journey to Mudryi.

FERTILE GROUND

During my participation with the healing group at the Foundation of Light, I discovered that acupuncture, homeopathic remedies, and hands-on healing were not the only methods of energetic healing. Light, sounds, and thoughts could also transmit healing energy.

Our meditation group examined the effect of musical tones on healing. One participant complained that she had experienced head and neck pain for two months. I played a note with a guitar, after which we chanted *om* to that tone for about one minute. Several tones were tried. We asked the participant with the head and neck pain how she felt following each one-minute chant. We discovered that when we chanted an om with a B-flat tone, her pain eased. We then proceeded to chant om in a B-flat tone for the next ten minutes, after which the participant exclaimed that her pain was gone.

During another session of our healing group at the Foundation of Light, a participant asked if we could help his mother. She was experiencing back pain. The interesting thing was she was in South Carolina, and we were in upstate New York. We chose to use him as a surrogate—someone who would represent the patient and actually receive treatment intended for the patient. We proceeded to use acupuncture points that were beneficial for back pain. He was not experiencing any back pain at the time he received the acupuncture. His mother was not informed prior to the procedure. The treatment lasted about a half an hour. At our next meeting, the surrogate reported that his mother, unaware of the treatment her son received, experienced a relief of her pain at the time he received acupuncture.

It is likely that this procedure did not cure her back pain, but it is an example of the possibilities of energetic healing and the profound effects it has, even when using a surrogate many miles away from the person experiencing pain.

These two accounts in the healing group gave momentum to my concept of energy's role in relieving a patient's suffering. These experiences also created the possibility that time and distance had little or no influence on the effectiveness of energetic healing.

Understanding the human energy field became a step on my journey. From my insights, if patients were healthy, their energetic fields were considered in balance. Balance in healing is thought of as an equilibrium or steadiness in the person's energy field. Healers would express this as, "The chakras are in balance; the meridians are in balance; the aura is in tune." If patients presented with an imbalance in their energy fields, they were considered energetically unstable or out of balance. As an acupuncturist, I could feel this in a patient's irregular pulse. I could see dark colors in the patient's aura or detect weakened energy in a patient's chakras with applied kinesiology.

I felt that the final explanation of the source of disease and healing was energetic healing by rebalancing the energetic field, aligning the chakras, and restoring a normal pulse, whether through the use of energetic therapies such as acupuncture or homeopathy or the results of the energy within an allopathic medicine. I continued study in chakra therapy, polarity therapy, applied kinesiology, and dowsing, looking to find the ultimate method that would produce healing. I felt that balancing energy through these various methods of healing would eventually lead me to a common source for healing. The journey to Mudryi became a path through the human energy field—and I saw a new context for illness.

WHY DO PEOPLE GET SICK?

For a time, I gave a lot of thought to the question, why do people get sick? I considered the possibility that there is something present within us that becomes out of balance before we become noticeably sick. I learned that in the middle of the nineteenth century, homeopathy used a hypothesis called *Hering's law of cure* to describe imbalances that existed in energetic bodies before physical manifestation of disease occurred. Traditional Chinese medicine has an organized system of understanding energy, which also gives a context for the relationship between physical and energetic changes that occur during sickness.

Rather than focusing on our physical bodies, energetic practitioners perceive the etheric body as the location where disease processes occur. Having an imbalance in their energy can make a person vulnerable to physical illness. So even before a person gets physically sick, his or her energies may be out of balance, and this imbalance can be sensed by the healer. The acupuncturist can sense this through the patient's pulse, and the energetic healer can sense the imbalance through applied kinesiology or perceiving the aura. If the disturbance is powerful enough or is present long enough, the distressed energy eventually spills over into our physical body, and we get sick.

How does the energy become imbalanced? As in the physical body, disturbances in the etheric body can result from trauma (including emotional and mental trauma), poor nutrition, stress, lack of exercise, and constitutional weaknesses that we inherited from our ancestors. Practitioners of energy healing see these harmful influences as making the patient susceptible to infection from viruses, bacteria, and fungi. Once the disturbance has manifested in the physical body, treating the energy of the patient, as well has his or her physical condition, can promote healing.

Stress is a harmful influence that can be seen as energetic in its nature. It is like an arrow that pierces our energy and disrupts its normal flow. Stress first manifests in our etheric bodies as an interference in the circulation of energy and then comes out in our physical bodies as illness. When our bodies and minds experience stress, it can be perceived in the form of thoughts, emotions, and feelings of anxiety or fatigue, all which can be seen as states of energy in our bodies. I have felt the imbalance of my energy that arises from very strong burdens, like highly charged or repressed emotions or challenging life situations when there is upset with my children, relationships, and illnesses. My patients bring stress with them to their dental appointments.

Hans Selye, in his book *The Stress of Life*,[3] relates the conversion of stress into diseases of the physical body. Dr. Selye is credited with describing the system whereby the body copes with stress. He describes this process as the development of a pathological state from ongoing, unrelieved stress. He introduced the theory that the endocrine system is the physical conduit of stress and identified it as the hypothalamic-pituitary-adrenal axis. Under stress, our glands produce and discharge hormones that help cope with stress, but the continual release of these hormones under chronic stressful conditions contributes to a weakening of our bodies. He described states of coping with stress as an "alarm state," a "resistance state," and an "exhaustion state," referring to glandular conditions when we are under stress. He introduced a concept of energy in his work through the description of these "reservoirs" of stress resistance that contain stress energy.

Dr. Selye opened a door between the physical states of stress and energy. We can join his work, with the ideas of energetic healing. From a Chinese medicine perspective, stress is an energetic phenomenon. In acupuncture practice, stress is seen as stagnant energy stuck in the body, and many of our modern health problems arise from these internal blockages. Acupuncturists view the body's energy as the first line of defense to prevent illness. Human beings have a protective energy called *wei chi*. The wei chi can be seen as a force field around our bodies. Other healers see this as our auras. When this protective force field is stressed, as it is in periods of anxiety and worry, most times our protective energy wards off the challenge. However, under unrelieved stress, we experience a weakening of the force field, leading to a failure in the stress-fighting mechanisms in our etheric bodies. The energy in our bodies becomes affected and, if not treated, can lead to physical disease.

Accordingly, stress is a form of energy that pierces our etheric bodies. These energetic changes can be detected and then treated through acupuncture and homeopathy before they manifest physically, based on symptoms such as fatigue, lack of mental clarity, anxiety or other emotional disturbances, pains in the body, and other indicators of imbalance.

A model depicting the nature of the energy field (etheric body) can be assembled from acupuncture, religion, and the work of Alice Bailey[4] and Richard Gerber.[5] All of these resources portray the etheric body as an invisible entity in and around the physical body. The knowledge contained in the etheric body is an unlimited resource for understanding life in the presence of health and disease. The following is a summation of what has been presented.

> The etheric body has organization and is not separate from the physical body. The etheric energy emanates from the physical body, analogous to light from a light bulb, and the quality of this energy can

be sensed by the healer through his or her intuitive skills.

➢ The condition of the human energetic field (the etheric body) is an indicator of health and disease in the human body. If the physical body experiences illness, then the energy in the etheric body will show this.

➢ Evaluation of the etheric body can be used to determine the energetic state of our organs and glands. For example, pulse diagnosis used by an acupuncturist or applied kinesiology used by an energetic healer can evaluate the organs and glandular systems in the body.

➢ Disease may be detected in the etheric body before signs of disease occur in the physical body. Energetic healers can sense these changes and work to direct the energy toward health.

➢ Imbalances of the etheric energy, as caused by stress, bring about disease in the physical body. The physical symptoms are healed through the restoration of balance in the etheric body with acupuncture, homeopathy, or the laying of hands.

➢ The etheric body has been diagramed by several healing systems, including meridians in Chinese medicine, chakras from the Vedic system of health, and auras from pre-Christian religions. Although their organization appears disconnected, the underlying purpose of restoring energetic balance remains the same.

THE JUMPING-OFF POINT

And then things changed. The perplexing thing was that I found that no one energetic system held the right method for healing all problems and for all patients. In my practice, I found that some patients would be helped by homeopathy, some by acupuncture, and some by medications.

The next question arose: "If energetic methods are not the universal source of healing, then what is the source?" Energy was a common factor, but focusing the energy through the various techniques of energetic healing did not always explain the results, especially when I discovered that no two practitioners of energetic healing diagnosed and practiced in the same way.

None of the techniques of energetic healing seemed to hold the ultimate answer to the mystery of the source of healing. I found that the energetic techniques I used worked for some conditions but not all and sometimes worked best in combination. I saw that some practitioners were more successful in their work than others—or so they claimed. On my journey, science, an analytical system based on inductive and deductive logic, was joined with a theory of energetic healing, and still I felt I had not arrived at the source of healing.

I received a certification to practice acupuncture in my dental practice. I studied acupuncture and related aspects of traditional Chinese medicine. Chinese medicine has systems of categorizing the manner in which health and disease manifest energetically in our physical bodies. The theories of the five elements and the eight factors were developed in Chinese medicine to describe the energetic manifestations, and they became part of my diagnostic practice. The five elements represent characteristics of nature that can be related to attributes and behaviors of the human being. Specifically, the elements are fire, earth, air (metal), water, and wood. In Chinese medicine, the patient is seen as influenced by one or more of these elements, and therapy is directed toward balancing the energy of the body.

I had an experience that would shift my thoughts to another possibility.

Over the next few years, as part of my studies, I met with practitioners who were very experienced in the practice of acupuncture and Chinese medicine. One particular acupuncturist, Hari Jot Singh, read my pulses and stated that I had had mononucleosis when I was nineteen years old—I was thirty-one at the time. I had experienced a severe case of mononucleosis at the age of nineteen! He had no prior knowledge of this, so how did he do this?

I discovered that Hari Jot Singh was capable of more than what traditional acupuncture taught. I didn't know what these skills were, but I was intrigued and moved to find the answer to this mystery. Maybe there was something other than the empirical methods of science, something other than the sensations and experience of the etheric body. Was there a connection between the healer and patient of which I was not aware?

Hari Jot Singh's special capabilities were a jumping-off

point for my studies in spirituality and the relationship of health and disease to religion and spirit. Energetic healing offered many explanations for healing but not the one that satisfied my yearning to get to the source of healing. When I looked at the world's major religions, they all espoused compassion, with a goal of freedom from suffering. Suffering and healing go hand in hand. Perhaps spirituality held the answer to the mystery of healing. I dove off into the discipline of spiritual life.

· · · · · · · ● ● ● ● ● ● ● ● ● ● · · · · ·

HEALING MEDITATION 3

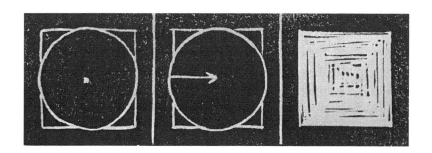

Contemplation is an activity of the soul, detached from the mind, while the mind is in a quiet state.

Compassion: Our practice on focusing to create the calm, peaceful listening that comes with the compassionate mind brings us to the possibility of experiencing a phenomenon that is found in many religious and meditative practices. This is the realm of the soul. Jung chose to describe this consciousness as our *active imagination.*

Using the practices found in Healing Meditations 1

and 2, at this point you are able to reach a state of calm and peace quite readily. Within this peace, the compassionate mind can observe what is present for you. Each of us will have a unique experience. One could say we are conscious of the emanations of the unconscious mind.

➢ Again, start where you are. There will be no special posture at this point. However, if you want to sit quietly, that is okay. Notice your mind, listen to your thoughts, and feel the sensations arising within you. Make no judgment, and do not fix on any one idea. This can be accomplished while standing, lying, sitting, or walking.

➢ Bring a focus to your mind. It may be a person who needs healing or a question that has come up in your life that has not been answered. Bring in a consciousness of the compassion and observe what is happening in your mind. In this state, the members of our healing group experience visions of colors or pastoral scenes. We hear the voice that comes from the silence, and we sense the energy around us. Remain in this state until an image is seen, a feeling is sensed, or a voice heard. These will be subtle impressions at first, so just observe. Return to your thoughts and note what was experienced. This lays the foundation for co-cognition. You have experienced a connection to the soul and have brought a message or guidance to your consciousness. Be with this.

The Zen of Healing

- When you can sense something without desire.
- When you help without needing payback,
- When you can be grateful for other people's experiences,
- When you can empathize with others' misfortunes,
- When you can hear another's suffering without suffering yourself,
- When you can be hungry and intelligently satisfy your hunger,
- When you can be lonely and understand its temporary nature,
- When you can feel hurt and pain and flow with its meaning,
- When you can sense beauty without desire,
- When you can see happiness and not question it,
- When you can accept personality for what it is,
- When you can desire without a sense of purpose or loss,
- Then you experience the peace in healing.

Ira Kamp

Chapter 4

Energy to Soul

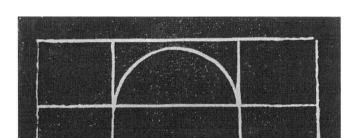

A friend of mine, Otis, shared the following story with me when we were talking about connection to our souls. I don't think he was aware of the impact that his story had on me, but maybe that is the way it was supposed to be.

Otis was running for exercise in his neighborhood. In the midst of a five-mile jaunt, a dog came out of nowhere and was aggressively biting at his legs. As he sped up in the hope of leaving the dog behind, he thought he heard the owner of the dog say "sic 'em," which meant more danger. From some unknown place inside Otis came an impulse, and he put his palm out to the dog and said "Peace!" The dog abruptly stopped his attack and began running alongside Otis, now jogging as a partner. Both Otis and the owner were in awe.

This story showed me the value of Otis's spontaneous reaction to a threat and the miracle that followed. I saw his spontaneity as his intuition coming through to guide his actions that pacified the dog. It was if Otis knew, and the dog knew. There was no time for contemplation. The wonder of intuition motivated me on my journey.

MISSING IN ACTION

Something was missing. Could it be that what I needed to continue on my journey was not some way of action but rather a new way of thinking? Hari Jot Singh's ability to know about my health history without his prior knowledge of an illness I had experienced twelve years earlier did not exist in my training or experience. My culture and education provided no context for my ability to know something about another person without conscious communication. Otis's experience with the dog showed me the possibility that something or someone, like an inner voice, is there to guide us, whether we are aware of its presence or not.

I noticed that my thinking was fixed in scientific

reasoning. My mind would not allow a change or a shift in my consciousness. It was like trying to put a square peg in a round hole. The peg was my thinking; the hole was the scientific paradigm in which I grew up and received my training. My mind had no space for this unexplained guidance to fit. I felt I needed to either change the hole or alter the peg. I knew that the hole (my culture and education) would not transform. The onus was on me to change my thinking.

Up to this point, my thoughts were the guidance for living my life. However, I was not able to experience a breakthrough in my thinking. The creation of a bridge between science and energetic healing turned out not to be my journey's destination. In fact, my mind was wound so tightly with thoughts that I felt like I was losing ground in my pursuit of the mystery of healing. Life lacked meaning and purpose; I was at an impasse.

I now know that this breakdown preceded a breakthrough on a very important step on my journey. Thomas Kuhn,[1] a modern physicist and philosopher, has written extensively on a paradigm's influence on advances in science. His main point is that what is accepted as reality depends upon the paradigm or an agreed-upon way of thinking. This is evident on an individual basis as well as in large groups, communities, and populations. So maybe there was an inherent truth outside of my consciousness that could enlighten me on my journey.

This was not the case.

MEDITATION AND HEALING

"Meditation means the gradual process of training the mind to focus … and to remain [present]. The constant practice of meditation helps one to develop a calm and concentrated mind and help to prepare one for the attainment of wisdom and enlightenment, ultimately."[2]

In an article in the *Scientific American* (2014),[3] the author states that about fifteen years of research has been done, which more than shows that meditation produces significant changes in both the function and structure of the brains of experienced practitioners. These studies are now starting to demonstrate that contemplative practices may have a substantive impact on biological processes critical for physical health.

Meditation was a major milestone on my journey to awakening to a new possibility in healing. I was first introduced to meditation while in college. What at first was a game played by my intellectual mind became a way of accessing the quiet parts of my being, where a world of wisdom resided. As I became involved in health care, meditation played a larger role in helping me stay calm in stressful times and helping to find meaning in an apparently chaotic world.

Meditation is a way of connecting our intellect to the soul. The focus of our minds makes available healing energy that benefits the person in need of healing. Through meditation, the healer's health benefits as well. I have found that the calm and focused experience in meditation gives me strength and relaxation during my work.

Meditation can be the basis for all forms of healing. Whatever healing methods we use, our techniques are enhanced by the centering and the awareness that comes from meditation. When in meditation, we can be the source of healing for maladies that are present not only in individuals but also in our communities and in the world. Our goals are only limited by what and how we think. Meditation moves us beyond our intellect into a consciousness based on balance and peace. Meditation transforms and enlightens us.

Once, while meditating, I realized that I would never find the road to my journey through experiences outside of my inner consciousness. All guidance and direction would come from within. Consequently, I gave up the idea that an angel would come and take me to enlightenment. Instead, I chose to go inward. Inner consciousness became my focus, and this led me to the discovery of my inner voice.

THE PENDULUM SWINGS INWARD

I needed a shift in my science and energy paradigms to another awareness that would solve the mystery of healing. Like a pendulum, my thoughts began to swing away from the external phenomenal world to a possibility of a consciousness within my mind. One of the greatest experiences on my journey to Mudryi was the discovery of my inner voice. In 1986, I met Mabel Beggs and Kate Payne, two of the founding members of the Foundation of Light in Ithaca, New York. They talked of reincarnation, angels, guides, and karma without any indication of disbelief. They were certain that there is an intelligence within our minds, separate from our own consciousness, that guides us, and this intelligence also has physical manifestations. They were emphatic that spiritual guides and angels exist. To be honest, I did not completely understand what they were talking about. I had heard of people receiving guidance from within their minds, but I had never experienced this guidance and never heard voices in my head except my own. I had never heard elders in my life, family, teachers, or friends speak this way. Could there be an intelligence that I could sense that would guide me by way of my thoughts? Maybe the angels that Kate and Mabel were speaking of did exist, and I could hear them. The possibility of having company in my consciousness was fascinating—and intrigued me to learn more.

And then I happened upon something totally outside my realm of possibility: finding my own inner voice. It was like discovering a new room in my house. A magical space, which probably had always been there, appeared.

I first realized that I was not alone within my personal consciousness while sitting beneath a waterfall near my office in Ithaca. My mind was filled with thoughts of how to fix my life so I could survive my challenges. I was stressed from starting a new practice and the arrival of a baby in our family. My thoughts were endlessly going round and round when suddenly a thought that had a distinctive voice came from somewhere in my mind and said something totally out of context. The voice spoke out above the myriad other thoughts crying out for attention, calmly saying, "Relax. Everything is okay." I responded repeatedly about how wrong life was, but the voice answered unswervingly, "Relax. Everything is okay." After about twenty minutes, I finally gave in, and the feeling of calmness overcame me.

At first, I felt like there might be something wrong with this. I thought, *This is crazy. Am I the only one who has had this type of conversation inside my mind? Am I the only one who is able to experience this?* Upon further contemplation, I came to the conclusion that if the ability to hear my own inner voice is possible, then everyone—and especially those serving patients—has the ability to awaken his or her inner voice. Healers have the ability to eliminate distracting thoughts, focus on their patients, become aware of their own source of inspiration, and use it in their work.

Helpers in the New Room

The next day while lying in bed, my inner voice spontaneously invited me to ask questions. I asked a question about the troubles I was having, and the voice replied that these problems were there to teach me and increase my awareness. This was a unique and inspiring idea for me at the time. I needed to experience these stressful circumstances to better understand who I am.

Next, I asked a question about challenges that the members of my family were experiencing. My inner voice answered, "Wait a minute. I have to check on something. Be back later." I waited with excitement yet calmness. My inner voice soon returned with an answer to my question. The message was clear: *What my family members are going through also is meant to help them to grow, to be wiser.*

There was one other question that I remember asking at the time—whether or not all people could communicate with themselves in this manner. The voice responded, "All persons are capable of experiencing a connection to their inner voice, a source for inspiration. In fact, we all are already connected with our inner voices, whether we are aware of it or not."

As a result of this discovery, I found that I had a choice in how I thought, and the possibility of choice opened new doors for discovery. While previously my thoughts were based on surviving my life's challenges, there now was space in my mind for creation—a freedom for self-expression not based solely on my thoughts of past experiences.

The experience of meeting my inner voice inspired me to continue on my journey. I could reach a calmness in my mind with meditation. Out of the calmness arose my inner voice that answered my questions about health and healing and framed my discoveries in ways that helped me develop and grow as a healer— recommendations appeared indicating which homeopathic remedies would be effective; what allopathic medicines would be beneficial, and which acupuncture points would be most indicated for treatment. Furthermore, knowing that I have a guiding voice inspired me to explore the possibility that all people could create a connection with their inner voices and use them in their work. I looked forward to sharing this experience with members of the Foundation of Light and using it in our healing group.

Somewhere in this, I had become stuck in a paradigm that created a division of life; science, energy, and spirit were separate. The discovery of my inner voice helped changed my perception. My inner voice inspired me toward another way of thinking. What came to me was something totally outside of my previous thoughts. It happened in an instant without my actively working on it. The practice of meditation and connection to my inner voice gave me the ability to choose the way I think, and I had a choice in the way I thought about science and spirituality.

SCIENCE AND SPIRITUAL PRACTICE

On my journey to Mudryi, the next step was my acknowledging the duality that existed in my thinking. I experienced my science and health care education as a system that promoted knowledge and stifled my beliefs and intuition. It fostered a separation of knowledge (objective thinking) and intuition (subjective thinking). I could think objectively, analyze data, and use scientific principles to pass my exams and balance my checkbook, and I could think subjectively, creating music and poetry. But there was a problem. For me, objective thought was my basis of learning science and my profession of dentistry. I valued this. On the other hand, my subjective thinking, which I used to create music and poetry, was overlooked by my profession. Subjective thinking was the source for my creativity and intuition but there was no place for that in my professional training. Furthermore, ideas such as life after death could not be explained by my objective thoughts. Bringing science and spiritual practice into the same arena was a challenge for me.

For me, science was based on objective knowledge, and this knowledge had not brought resolution to my quest to find the source of healing. Belief held some answers but failed in its attempts to blend with science. This created, in my mind, a dualistic way of thinking. I thought, *Beliefs have their place but not in the realm of scientific knowledge, and I know that I cannot balance my checkbook without objectivity.*

However, Eva Pierrakos, a spiritual teacher and founder of the Pathwork Foundation, has a different way of thinking about this duality. She commented on the duality of science and spirit: "While ... in this duality, it is impossible to experience and accept the realization that life brings both."[4] Life brings both the opportunity for objective knowledge and the opportunity for belief. She created the possibility of a fundamental philosophy that unified objective knowledge and belief—science and spirit.

In order to see beyond the duality of science and spirit, I would have to first think of them as one.

THE TEST

Creating my unified paradigm of science and spirit was put to the test. How could my healing work in dentistry bring together objective and subjective information? I took this quandary and my inner voice into my practice to test it out. A surprise was awaiting.

Katherine was in my office for a surgical procedure. One of the roots of her tooth did not respond to root-canal therapy, and I decided that I could remove the root and save the remaining tooth. She brought her daughter Leah, two years old at the time, because she could not find child care. She asked if she could hold Leah in her lap during the treatment.

"As long as she is calm and kept still," I told her, "she can remain in your lap." During the procedure, an interesting thing happened. For some reason, out of my concern for the comfort of my patient Katherine, I could hear within my mind the voice of Leah (although Leah was not physically speaking). Leah gave me clear directions on how to proceed in the surgery. She told me to let go of worrying about Katherine's comfort during the procedure. She would take care of that. Leah's voice spoke as if it was my thoughts coming through the voice of a two-year-old girl, and this two-year-old knew my skills. I was guided in the procedure to expose the root, cut the root off, and then suture the gum. I listened and followed her guidance. The guidance created a peace within me. The procedure went well, and Katherine healed without complications.

What I knew and how I thought led Katherine's treatment. However, I became aware that my intellect was not alone in her care. Rather, something beyond my intellect guided the treatment—my past experiences of my inner voice. It was a distinct voice, separate from my intellect, and Leah's voice felt like it came from the same place. I was thinking about what Osho[3] said about intuition: "When the Soul functions spontaneously, that is called intuition." From this, the idea of soul came to my mind. I did not really understand what soul was at that time, but I looked at the possibility that my inner voice was soul talking to me, guiding me.

The discovery and exploration of soul were the next steps on my journey.

THE SOUL IN SIMPLE TERMS

For me, the soul was a mystery. I had heard the word soul described time and time again, but soul still remained unclear. Soul was written about extensively by spiritual and religious leaders, but the exact meaning of soul remained elusive for me. I assumed that people throughout the entire world knew what soul was. Somewhere along the line, I'd just missed it. The word did describe my spiritual nature, but I did not experience my soul until I stopped looking for it outside of myself.

An idea came to me: *My soul is as plain as the end of my nose. It was right in my face all this time.* Soul was something that was just present in my consciousness, and I did not have to study or search for it. Soul revealed itself to me through words. I could hear soul through my inner voice; it was the way my soul related to me. At the time, of course, "me" was my intellect.

It didn't take Otis long, nor did he need complicated maneuvers, to produce his result of being safe when he confronted the dog. His action seemingly came from a source within him, no questions asked, no prayer being said. I saw Otis's response as arising from soul and giving him an ability to connect with the dog.

Looking back at my experiences with Katherine's treatment, I found that my soul was accessed through my focused thoughts and intentions. Focus was the first step. Focus, for me, created an intention of connection and compassion for my patient. I also felt that this intention had priority over any chosen method of healing. I came to know soul as an easily recognized faculty of my consciousness that could be accessed at any moment.

Simply stated, soul appears as a voice, a feeling, and/or vision that arises out of the silence of mindfulness. I believe that all human beings have the capacity to be conscious of their souls. It just takes accepting that soul is there. The expression of soul arises from our inner beings and not from a source seen, heard, or felt outside of our consciousness.

Our intellect's main interest is to manipulate, possess, and grasp. "Unless mind knows everything, it remains afraid—because knowledge gives power. If there is something mysterious, you are bound to remain afraid because the mystery cannot be controlled."[4] However, I can acknowledge my judgments, my fears, and my thoughts that have the intention to control life, rather than share life. They do come from within me but are unconnected, independent, and distinct from the voice of my soul.

Soul appears when we stop thinking. Stop the mind, the reasoning, and the logic, and silence happens. In soul consciousness, our nervous systems are not stimulated through one or more of the five senses; rather, something is understood from within. For me, soul manifests as a guiding voice, and I can distinguish the voice by listening for the qualities of kindness, compassion, and guidance with positive actions.

Out of the stillness, soul rises like the phoenix out of the ashes. It opens a world of creativity, peace, and wisdom that connects us to everything in the universe.

HEALING MEDITATION 4

ILLUMINATION: LISTENING WITH OUR COMPASSIONATE MINDS

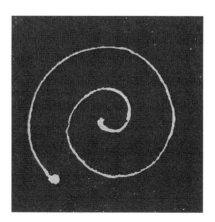

Illumination is receiving guidance from the soul. With meditation, we can become aware of the guidance and its meaning for those on whom we are focusing for healing. To review, in Meditation 1, a discipline of focus was developed. In Meditation 2, the practice of prolonged focus was developed. In Meditation 3, from the silence that is created while we are in meditation, messages are received.

The fourth step involves recognizing the guidance we receive during meditation. We continue to be in the peaceful space of the compassionate mind. Now our mental processes will focus on creating meaning from the messages.

> Sit quietly, focus your mind, and bring the intention of healing with you.
> Once you are mindful of the silence, wait for words, visions, or feelings to appear.
> Observe these words, visions, or feelings that arise. These are the messages from your soul. Usually, one of these emerges but you may experience all three.
> Become totally absorbed in the experience. Be aware that what you experience may be figurative or representative of what you know.
> Continue in the peaceful state that arises with the compassionate mind and the message will illuminate your consciousness with the guidance that will inspire your work.
> Remember the words, feelings, or visions. These are the communications of your soul.
> Then return to the part of your mind that has the ability to analyze the message received.
> Then contemplate actions based on the guidance.

CHAPTER 5

INTELLECT AND INTUITION:
A WAY TO SOUL

*If you want, come in. Do not stand outside; no
explanation is possible from the inside to the
outside. Some come in—be an insider.*
—the Upanishads

Our intellect and intuition are remarkable attributes, and
so much time has been spent contemplating them. I feel
it would be helpful if we spent a little more time on their
distinctions.

Intellect and Intuition

Before going into how we receive guidance from soul, it is important to understand the nature of how we think and intuit. Our intellect is a wondrous tool with which we gather and organize information to build our basis of knowledge. Our intuition is a glorious tool that gives us the ability to receive information without knowing it first.

We discover and understand information by means of the intellect. The intuition creates information without the need of a knowledge base. Intellect and intuition stand on either side of a bridge. The bridge starts to form when we discover the distinction between the intellect and intuition. The bridge is complete when we can value and use both in our everyday lives.

Besides our instinctual behaviors, human beings express themselves in three ways: the intellect, the personality, and the intuition.

Intellect

Intellect is the ability to reason or understand or to perceive relationships and differences. It is the power of the mind manifested through thought. Intellect is a conscious state created by our thinking process, combined with our sensual process (the senses and emotions). It may be positive or negative in its effect.[1]

The ability to think may not be unique to human beings, but the depth and the creative nature of our thoughts sets us apart from other species. Alice Bailey states, "To many the achievement of intellectual ability is the consummation of the work of evolution."[2]

Osho writes, "Intellect is human. All our sciences, all our businesses, all our professions, whatever is going on in the world—our politics, our religion, our philosophy— they are based on intellect. Intellect is human."[3]

All of us have varying degrees of intellect or the capacity to think and reason. For some of us, however, thinking is instinctual. Our primary concerns are about survival, food, shelter, money, and relationship. With our intellect, we can rise above our instinctual behaviors; and our thoughts can be focused on achieving freedom from the burdens that life has given us.

Creativity combined with our sensual processes and emotions and the capacity to think forms the intellect. The intellect is what we identify ourselves with, and with this information we create our physical world.

The intellect's strength lies in a definition of life that inspires us to build and continue to construct a life, a community, or a civilization that grows with predictability. It organizes things so that they can be reproduced. The intellect records life, so we can connect with history. The intellect categorizes information so that we can distinguish between what works and what doesn't. The intellect allows us to balance our checkbook.

There is one more attribute of the intellect that needs to be mentioned: the intellect is not closed off to our intuitive nature, and, for most of us, the intellect requires training to be in touch with the intuition.[4]

Personality

The expression of our intellect and emotions is called the *personality*. In particular, the intellect is like a pump, pushing thoughts, emotions, and feelings into our being, coloring the personality. When we are solely conscious with our intellectual nature, our personality is based on interactions in the material world. Within its consciousness of the material world, the intellect functions on the basis of scientific and empirical data. This information, along with our experiences, builds the foundation of our knowledge so that everything we know is built upon a former idea that the personality feels has been proven to be true.

On the positive side, our intellect brings the development and construction of an organized physical world, including technological advances in health care, providing organized health care to billions of people. On the negative side, if we use our intellect without the intuition (based on compassion), our thoughts and actions tend toward intolerance and materialism. For example, I commonly hear from my patients that in the dental offices they previously visited their problems were seen as a way for the dentists to make money. The patients frequently were overtreated.

We see and describe physical objects through our intellect, but there is another source that influences our personality. It is a force that is creative but not creative in the physical sense. The source arises from an unconscious place—or at least a place that our intellect calls unconscious. The way that ideas and experiences come to us spontaneously is called the *intuition*.

Intuition

Intuition is the ability to perceive or know things without conscious reasoning. It is a conscious state that arises from our creative potential (soul and spirit). It may be positive or negative in its effect. Intuition cannot be explained scientifically because the very phenomenon is unscientific and irrational. And intuition is something beyond the intellect, something not of the intellect, something coming from someplace where intellect may not be aware. So, the intellect can be conscious of it, but the intellect can find it difficult to explain.[5]

Myers and Briggs[6] write that people who prefer to use intuition pay the most attention to impressions or the meaning and patterns of the information. Intuitive people would say I'm interested in new things and what might be possible so that I think more about the future than the past. I like to work with symbols or abstract theories, even if I don't know how I will use them. I remember events more as an impression of what it was like than as actual facts or details of what happened. The following statements generally apply to me:

- I remember events by what I read "between the lines" about their meaning.
- I solve problems by leaping between different ideas and possibilities.
- I am interested in doing things that are new and different.
- I like to see the big picture; then find out the facts.

- I trust impressions, symbols, and metaphors more than what I actually experienced.
- Sometimes I think so much about new possibilities that I never look at how to make them a reality.

With intuition, a person perceives more than what is there, more than a physical object, more than what is thought and felt. I believed that developing my intuition was an important step on my journey.

The following are two of my observations of intuition:

➢ At a meeting I was attending at the Foundation of Light, one of the participants, Jane, was a psychotherapist. She told a story about being with a client, and before the client spoke, Jane saw a goldfish in her mind. Without prompting, the client sadly said she had a tank of fish and all had died except one.

➢ At another healing class, a participant, Margaret, spoke about her life. I looked at her, and inside my head I saw a turtle. A short time later, Margaret said she felt she was in a shell, referring to being afraid to come out into the world.

INTUITION: THE SIXTH SENSE

When reason fails, only intuition can work.
—Osho

Osho says it best—that intuition cannot be explained rationally. But I will try anyway. Intuition comes from the word "tutor," or to be taught. In a spiritual context, intuition allows all experiences to be part of our lesson because it can contact the light in all physical forms with a sense of equality and compassion.[7]

We think of intuition as a magical experience, but it is part of human nature. Intuition is a sense, one that all human beings have. In fact, it can be called our *sixth sense*. We use our five senses of hearing, sight, taste, touch, and smell to interact, assess, and react to the physical world. We use our sixth sense, intuition, to interact with the realm we can call the unconscious or superconscious world. The intuition is a capacity of human beings, the use of which can produce a thriving life. As Alice Bailey writes, "The man who is successful is the man who can think, and who can utilize the sixth sense, the mind [intuition], to produce certain specific results."[8]

Bailey stresses that intuition is a normal, useful state for everyone:

> The development of spiritual perception and illumined intellect can be part of the equipment of the sane and balanced businessman or scientist and need not necessarily indicate a lack of psychic balance or emotional instability. The light of illumination and of inspiration [Intuition] is quite compatible with the pursuit of one's daily occupations.

Intuition and Healing

Intuition is one way that a person can perceive life, but it is not the only way in which we see our world. According to Jung, there are four psychological characters of human consciousness: thinking type, feeling type, using sensations type, and using intuition type.

We can perceive the world with a combination of these psychological types, but according to Jung, only one predominates. I have observed that healers, including me, are predominantly of the intuitive type.

On my journey, my experiences pointed to the use of intuition in energy healing. The other three types of psychological characters, thinking, sensations and feeling helped in my understanding of the physical world. The technical thoughts that I use in my work, the awareness of the body's response to the treatments I provide to my patients, and the sensitivity to the feelings of my patients are invaluable tools in my practice of dentistry. However, my intuition gave me access to the realm of soul. I discovered that meditation is a good promoter of intuitive qualities and I could use the meditation techniques that I knew to foster my intuition and experience soul.

What the intellect lacks is the capacity to explain ideas such as death, God, spirit, soul, and reincarnation. Alice Bailey describes our lack of awareness in these areas:

> We are conscious of a profound dissatisfaction with physical life as a whole, and with our inability to grasp and

understand the divine reality which we hope exists. But it remains for us a matter for faith, and we want certainty. Life of the sense does not seem to carry us far enough along the path toward our goal.[9]

When the life of the senses falls short, this is where our intuition is necessary. It is through the intuition that we have the possibility to access the soul. We can receive information that guides us in our healing.

We can look at intuition, as well as the other senses, as a tool. Intuition is an ability to acquire information without needing literal definitions of the subject. In healing, the intuitive information gathered can be for the evaluation and treatment of the patient. The information comes to the healer, and, responding, the healer puts his or her skills into action.

Mona Lisa Schulz, MD, PhD, in her book *Awakening Intuition*,[10] writes:

> Intuitive insights are hard to describe in words, or more accurately, they reveal themselves as a gestalt, as hunches that are difficult to put words to. The left brain, however, quickly begins to fill in words and details, making the intuition marketable and easy to communicate.

The use of our intuition can be seen in applied kinesiology, dowsing, and other forms of alternative healing. These methodologies function by giving the healer access to the energy body of the patient. While interacting with the patient's energy body, using applied kinesiology and intuition, the healer discerns the condition of the patient and the treatment that will help. As I have shown with AK testing, the diagnostic and therapeutic locations tested on the body are given their meaning by the healer. Since the areas of testing with AK vary in name and meaning, it is a perfect place to use intuition.

INTUITION AS OUR GUIDE

At the age of ten, my daughter, Rachel, had a chronic cough for three months, and medical treatment was not effective at healing it. I had recently learned about the seven-star hammer (an instrument used in the practice of acupuncture) from a colleague, Dr. Jin Fang. The theory goes like this: if there is congestion in the chest, the seven-star hammer can be used on the patient's back to bring the congested chi to the surface. This would eliminate the congestion and health would ensue. I proceeded to treat Rachel. The seven-star hammer is an actual hammer with seven needles embedded on the hammer head. The hammer is tapped gently on the skin in the thoracic area on the patient's back along the spinal column. The action of the hammer causes an irritation on the skin. Sometimes the skin bleeds during the therapy, but this is seen as the removal of stagnant energy and therefore is a good sign.

I used the seven-star hammer one evening. The next morning, Rachel awoke with a rash on her back in the area of treatment. At first glance, it looked like poison ivy, but it was the middle of winter, and that was not possible. The next thought that struck me was that she had shingles. Shingles is a viral infection caused by the same virus as chicken pox.

Rachel had had a very mild case of chicken pox when she was three. However, her illness did not produce enough immunity to this virus, so she was susceptible to reinfection. Shingles manifests as crusty and painful lesions on the skin. Well, this was crusty, and the pain—severe pain—came on later that day. She was seen by her physician and a homeopath, both of whom agreed that Rachel had shingles. Coincidentally, I had just taken a healing class with Nicki Scully, an experienced healer and teacher. She based her work on the teaching of an Egyptian god of healing, Thoth. We were instructed in and experienced the use of animal thought forms in healing. I chose one such animal—a snake—in my attempts to heal Rachel. She already had Tylenol 3 in her but was still experiencing severe pain. I lay next to her, and the snake came to mind. I proceeded to "wrap" the snake around her body, tightly, with no gaps. Remember—the snake arose from my imagination, but I went through the motions of surrounding her body with the snake as if it physically existed. Immediately, I observed Rachel becoming calm and falling asleep. She would wake up after a few hours, and I would repeat the wrapping, and she would become calm and return to sleep. The next morning, my wife and I witnessed something we will never forget. In the midst of the shingles lesions on Rachel's back there were two red spots about an eighth of an inch apart that looked like a snake bite! We took this as an affirmation of the healing that was taking place. The seven-star hammer was not used again. Rachel continued to have pain, but whenever I imagined the snake around her body, her pain diminished. It took about a week for her to fully recover. How could this happen—and with such dramatic results?

The intuition is capable of seeing into objects, such as a human body, and bringing out what is hidden within. Jung concurs with this.[11] His explanation of the intuitive psychological type points out that the intuition seeks to find the possibility in the object. The intuitive healer works from this perspective. In the context of healing, the intuition of the healer looks "into" the patient but not just the physical body. With his or her intuition, a healer can sense the state of the energy in the body and, with this information, proceed with the appropriate therapy. Intuitively, the healer will sense energy as normal, in excess, or deficient. The healer intuitively searches far and wide and shallow and deep for information that lies within the patient. The healer "looks" for areas where energy is sufficient or deficient (light or darkness) within the physical form. The energy is perceived by the healer as a vision or thought or by an initial sensation or feeling. These perceptions then guide the healer in his or her work. Rachel gave this to me.

Jung found that permanently embedded and constant in the unconscious human mind are personifications called *archetypes*. Some examples are the Orphan, the Hero, the Caregiver, the Rebel, the Sage, and the Magician. The archetypes that we carry define who we are and affect our thinking and behavior. We are unconscious of the influences of the archetypes unless we work on uncovering their identities through psychological counseling.

The archetypes can also be uncovered through meditation and intuition. In our healing meditations, we focused upon the patient. After the meditation, the healers recounted what they heard, felt, or visualized—a description of a concept, object, thought, feeling, or other sensation. We came to explain this as an intuitive association with the patient's archetype. Out of this relationship, the healer gained insights. These insights contained the guidance that was used in healing. My experience with my daughter and the snake is a good example of this process. Out of my meditation arose the image of a snake. I knew what the snake meant, and I used it to guide my actions to relieve her pain.

Over time, it became clearer to me that there is more to my thoughts and knowledge than whatever I am conscious of. The idea of a personal inner guide came to me from my own intuition, not from a teacher or book. I had no earlier occasion for contemplation on the matter. It was spontaneous.

I believe that we can access our intuition, and in fact we are always in communication with our intuition, albeit unconsciously. The primary hurdle is to trust and listen consciously. When I choose to live a conscious life, aware of my inner guidance, transformation and healing are more likely to occur. The path of life transforms from suffering into a life of peace and healing.

At the Foundation of Light healing group, we found that using intuition as our guide can motivate healers into a way of practicing that helps reduce stress and suffering in our patients. And the practice of healing does not stop there. The desire for relieving the suffering in our patients expands into a need to heal all who suffer in the world. Global healing becomes a focal point in healers' lives.

ACTIVE IMAGINATION

Discovering and developing our intuition is possible. Jung identified the ability of the mind to awaken to our intuition as *active imagination*, a process by which we place our imaginary power into a given situation. The active imagination is different from the imagination that produces fantasy or unreal information. Fantasy is illusion that limits our minds to places where there is little or no possibility for our ideas to manifest in the physical world. In these fantasies, we become mainly concerned about our own personal thoughts and feelings. The fantasies may be about the creation of great things, such as world peace or the end of hunger, but there is no avenue for their manifestation, only our desire to feel better about the situation.

Active imagination is a cognitive methodology that uses the imagination as an organ of understanding. As developed by Carl Jung between 1913 and 1916, active imagination is a meditation technique wherein the contents of one's unconscious are translated into images, narrative, or personified as separate entities. It can serve as a bridge between the conscious mind and the unconscious mind and includes working with dreams and the creative self via imagination. Jung associated active imagination with oneness and inter-relatedness consciously put together from a set of fragmented and dissociated parts.[12]

Active imagination can be used to train the intellect to work with the intuition by focusing the imagination on a subject and taking meaning from what arises in the imagination. Active imagination is a way to develop our intuition for situations that need our help, understanding, compassion, direction, or healing. It enables the healer to gather the wisdom of the patient's unconscious mind and receive guidance.

The use of active imagination promotes a collaboration of the intellect and intuition. Specifically, in healing—as Jung alludes—it is a way of bridging our intellect and intuition. At the Foundation of Light healing group, new members were introduced to intuition with the use of their imaginations. This was especially helpful for participants unfamiliar with intuition; they used their imagination, although sometimes reluctantly. Many said that their imaginations had been strong in their childhoods. As adults, the imagination is not so valued, and so it is not frequently called upon.

Leading up to the healings, we would sit in a circle, with the patient lying in the middle of the circle. Then I would direct the healers of our group in a guided meditation. The intent was to connect with the patient through our meditation and use our imaginations. I would first have them imagine a light in their heads just above the eyes in the center. This light could be imagined as a flame, a light bulb, a window with sunlight shining through, or a feeling of lightness. This light, I would tell them, was their soul, and in this place, they could use their imaginations and observe what came to their consciousness. Following the meditation, which lasted ten minutes, the healers would share their experiences. They would report visions of light over the patient, scenes with the patient in nature, sensations of specific areas of the patient's body, and words describing the patient's condition.

After practicing with the active imagination, healers can recognize this as their intuition. It becomes familiar and easily accessed. Once learned, our intuition, the sixth sense, is like riding a bicycle. The skill remains with you.

SYMBOLS AND METAPHORS

Knowing the nature of the language of intuition was an important breakthrough on my journey to Mudryi. It began with this writing from Alice Bailey:

> It is realized that all forms are only symbols of an inner or spiritual reality, and spiritual reading involves the development

of the faculty of "reading" or seeing the life aspect which the outer form veils and hides. [Intuition is] reading with the eyes of the Soul, with the inner vision alert to find out that which is sought.[13]

Alice Bailey feels it is imperative for the healer to understand how the intuition reveals itself. Whereas intellect tends to function on the basis of scientific or empirical data, intuition is a gatherer of symbols and metaphors. Symbols and metaphors are objects and concepts that represent, stand for, or suggest ideas, visual images, beliefs, or actions that would otherwise not be associated with what is experienced. In healing with the use of intuition, it is important to realize that we are working with symbols and metaphors, and the symbols are unique to each person's intuition.

I now understood the mystery of the contrasted information received by healers with the same patient or same condition. The seemingly inconsistent conclusions reached during the healing courses I took and the various ideas gathered during our meditations in our healing group at the Foundation of Light could be explained through intuition, symbols, and metaphors. In the context of working with intuition, symbols and metaphors depict what the healer, using intuition, receives from the patient. However, the meaning of symbols and metaphors lies in the eyes of the beholder. A symbol received by one healer will rarely be the same for another. And if the symbol is similar, their interpretation of the symbol will not be the same.

Intuition was a determining step on my journey. Intellect and intuition are important partners in healing. The information received by a healer's intuition is in symbolic form. The intellect's role is to identify, translate, and relate these symbols to what is happening to the patient. The symbols are transformed by the intellect into useful information that guides the healer in the treatment of the patient.

One of the dental residents approached me with a concern: her patient was so anxious that she would not allow the resident to treat her painful tooth. When I first saw the patient, I could see she was struggling to be cooperative. She could not be still. She was seventeen years old, and even at a young age, she had a long history of traumatic dental experiences. For example, she would not be numb enough for a procedure and would suffer through it in pain. I sat quietly with her and held her hand. I was guided to ask her about music and her freedom to choose to be treated or not. She responded that she wanted to have the treatment done. She loved country music but thought we probably did not have it. Well, I did find some country music. I guided the resident on how to effectively apply local anesthesia to the affected tooth. I returned ten minutes later to find the patient was lying very still in the chair, enjoying the music while receiving root-canal treatment.

INTUITION AND SOUL

The human psyche is composed of three divisions: the conscious, the subconscious, and the superconscious mind, each having a unique and equally important duty and purpose. The conscious mind works through the five senses, giving us connection to the physical and phenomenal world. The subconscious mind is an unaware place in our minds that holds our thoughts and desires. The superconscious mind is an unaware place in our minds that is a reservoir of wisdom, creativity and connection, which generates compassion, innovation, and love. Even though we are generally unaware of the subconscious and superconscious minds, we can work to become conscious of them. It was the superconscious mind that inspired the next steps on my journey. The following story, written by a physician, exemplifies the superconscious mind used in healing.

My first experience with intuitive knowing helped me to save one of my patients' lives. It was during training, and I was having difficulty accessing the radial artery of a patient in shock. He was clamped down, and I could not thread the guide wire. After many futile attempts, I felt so frustrated, knowing that this critical step was necessary to get good data to save my patient's life. I don't know what came over me, but I suddenly stepped back from his bed and closed my eyes. A sense of peace came over me. I heard myself in my mind ask for guidance, for help. I don't know who I was asking, but I felt as though there was a response, a voice that said, "Go ahead." I thanked the voice and felt energized and reassured. I opened my eyes and stepped up to the patient. Without doubt, hesitation, or difficulty, I was able to access the patient's radial artery immediately. This helped me to turn the patient around at a crucial time. He eventually walked out of the hospital. It felt as though my hand was guided into the right place by an external force, and this phenomenon gave me a sense of amazement and awe. This was the first time I really felt connected to another level, a benevolent force. Since then, I've felt this guidance many, many times when helping to provide solutions to my patients. I firmly believe we have access to a whole other level in order to help each other, and I believe that our universe is indeed a friendly place that we create on an ongoing basis.[14]

Jung refers to the superconscious mind as the soul. Yogananda states that the superconscious mind is the all-knowing power of the soul that perceives truth directly—intuition. The soul is the individualized reflection of ever-existing, ever-conscious, ever-new joy, confined within the body of each and every being.[15]

Both Yogananda and Jung propose that the superconscious mind and the soul are one and the same. The founders of the Foundation of Light knew this and guided new members in how to connect with their souls through meditation. Kate Payne and Mable Beggs fervently felt a connection to soul. They would tirelessly teach it in study groups, meditations, and celebrations. All events began with meditation, even our board meetings. Naturally, soul connection became the groundwork of our healing group.

In our healing group, we found that a person could train his or her mind to use intuition. Initially, we found that intuition could be developed through the active imagination. For example, the participants would sit for a short time until an image, voice, or sensation arose. The meditation would be kept short so that each one could focus and speak about his or her experience. After several repetitions, the participants became comfortable in using their imaginations. This process would be redefined as accessing the intuition. It could be accessed and used easily and quickly.

Another example of a simple way of getting people to understand this was by pointing out that they could focus on the feelings they got from their hearts. Rollin McCraty,

PhD, director of research, HeartMath Research Center, states,

> Intuition is a process by which non-local information, normally outside the range of conscious awareness, is immediately sensed and perceived by the body's psychophysiological systems. It is not based on reason, logic, memories or extrapolations from the past. Experience of intuition is not confined to cognitive perception, but primarily involves the heart and the entire psychophysiological system.[16]

I take the possibility of using intuition with me to a place where I teach dentists in an advanced general dentistry program in Rochester, New York. The dentists come from all over the world: India, Pakistan, Iran, Romania, China, Colombia, Ecuador, Mexico, Canada, and a few from the United States. I call it the United Nations of Dentistry. It is a mixed culture of human beings learning how to better serve their patients. I receive many questions on how to treat specific conditions, as well as requests for recommendations for the treatment of their patients. Sometimes I ask what they feel in their hearts about the matter. It takes them to another dimension in their beings. I feel that focusing on their hearts instead of their minds opens the residents to their superconscious minds.

Karem, a resident from Colombia, was challenged by one of her patients. She was having difficulties in finding the right treatment plan for her patient, who experienced pain when chewing. She had to choose one of many options, including removing teeth, orthodontic treatment, and dentures. Most of us rely on our knowledge base to make decisions. However, this time I asked her what felt right, pointing her in the direction of using her heart rather than using her mind. All of a sudden, a lightness came about her. She said she felt the right way to go was orthodontic treatment. She had some experience as an assistant to an orthodontist, so her choice did have some knowledge behind it.

Intuitive perception, according to Jung, is a function of the conscious mind, and it is a way to understand the hidden truths within our superconscious minds and those of our patients. Jung proposes that the superconscious mind, the light, the soul, and the universal mind are one and the same. According to Jung, the superconscious mind has the desire to be understood by the conscious mind. He goes further, stating that a balance between the superconscious, conscious, and unconscious minds is a key to mental health.

Soul can be defined as the basic underlying consciousness in all beings. When the intuition is functioning, there is no sense of separateness between the self-consciousness of the intellect and soul. The connection creates a common sense of love, compassion, and intelligent use of will. Alice Bailey writes,

> Through the intuition we can become aware and experience universal consciousness. It is the intuition which reveals true Being and which induces a state of spiritual perception. We are able to understand the ways of universal consciousness in the world; and the ways of universal consciousness are revealed through the intuition.[17]

Soul, at first, appears to be intangible. It is perceived by our minds but does not seem to have a physical existence. I believe soul first comes to us as a mental concept of our spiritual nature through stories and movies. We spend a lot of time searching, trying to find an experience of soul. We take pilgrimages, think a lot, study, and take classes in pursuit of an experience of soul. Much of my time was spent looking for a connection to soul outside of me. I kept a disciplined eye out for an experience of angels, ghosts, nature devas—anything that would verify my concept of spirit and soul. I would hear stories from other people about seeing angels, and I wanted my own story to give myself confidence in the existence of the spiritual world. It never came, and I grew frustrated.

One afternoon, I sat in the woods on a hill behind the clinic where I worked and began meditation. My inner voice came into my consciousness, saying I would not find my soul by looking outside. The spiritual life and connection to soul lay within me. Give up the search outside and look inward. After that day in the woods, my journey took an inner path. I gave up the struggle to find spiritual validation outside my own consciousness.

Previously, I had found myself wanting to relate to the spirit and soul through my body—feeling it, seeing it, touching it, hearing it. After my meditation experience, I realized that body is physical in its nature and is bound by five senses. Experience of soul would have to come to me through another sense.

CHAPTER 6

SOUL AND HEALING

In all cultures, there is a reservoir of wisdom in what has been called our *super-consciousness* that is accessible within each of our minds. This wisdom is found in the Torah, the Koran, the Bhagavad Gita, and the Tao. The intuition, using active imagination, provides the pathway needed to bridge the superconscious and conscious mind. It connects our souls to our everyday lives.

When my son, Reuben, was nine years old, he experienced a severe headache while we were visiting my aunt. He was suffering horribly, but I had no access to acupuncture needles or any other medication to help him. He lay in bed in the dark while I sat next to him, wondering what I could do. Seeing my son suffer was a painful experience for me. I'd had migraine headaches as a kid, and I could feel his pain. I began meditation, and gently my inner guidance directed me to touch certain acupuncture points on his body with my right index finger. I held my finger on the point until the guidance told me it was enough. By the time I got to the fifth point, he was asleep; it was a miracle!

The combination of my knowledge of acupuncture and the guidance I received from my intuition created a healing for my son. His suffering was relieved, as well as my own worry about his suffering.

However, something was different in Reuben's healing. I noticed that the guiding voice was not my inner voice speaking. It sounded more like Reuben's voice. Reuben was unaware of the process, yet it was his voice. I had not experienced this with any of my previous healing work. Could it be that the information I received was not the guidance from my soul? I contemplated this discovery and concluded that my son unconsciously had guided me.

On my journey to Mudryi, I learned that our souls are the true source of healing energy. However, I spent two decades exploring the energetic basis for disease and healing before I was able to fully understand the soul's contribution in healing. My ability to relieve Reuben's suffering was among many experiences that convinced me there was something credible about energetic and spiritual healing. But at this point, it was not only my soul that was involved in the work. It seemed that the soul of the patient had an integral part in the healing work.

TAKING STOCK

Let's review where we have come on our journey. Three concepts bring light to my journey and also add further questions:

> A healer can gather vital information without speaking to the receiver.

It took me fifteen years of study, experience, and practice to understand how dentistry and acupuncture could be used together effectively. I felt confident about the integration of dental medicine and energetic healing methods, but there were a few more doors to open before my destination was reached.

One mystery that still puzzled me was how healers could know things about a person with whom they were working if they hadn't yet discussed that topic. I had been to several complementary healers who had this ability, and I could not logically understand it. The acupuncturist, who intuited that I had mononucleosis at the age of nineteen, had based his statement solely on reading my pulses when I was thirty-one years old. Remember—I had never told him about my illness! I had known Hari Jot Singh for a while and knew him to be an honest and compassionate person. He had been practicing for many years, and his talents as a healer were well known. Still, how could he know about my medical history without ever seeing me previously as a patient, without questioning me before he read my pulses, and without having access to my medical records?

> It is possible to have effective treatment for the same condition using different modalities.

As a participant in workshops led by healers trained in a variety of approaches to energetic healing, I noticed another paradox. Each system of energetic healing had its own way of assessing health and disease and specific therapies to treat a given condition. Yet each of these healing systems was professed by their practitioners as having resulted in successful therapy for the people receiving the healing. The successes were anecdotal, however, and could not be verified. The experience, training, and certification of the speakers was assumed to be enough for verification. For instance, in the diagnosis and treatment of TMJ pain and dysfunction, with all the various techniques in healing—acupuncture, homeopathy, hands-on healing, craniosacral therapy, and nutrition—the claim of success was very common in the courses that I attended. It did not seem logical or very scientific. The question was, how could such distinct systems with different approaches all have success when healing the same condition?

> ➤ What is the meaning behind the diversity of language in healing traditions?

The relationships among soul, energy, and language were central on my journey. I felt that both science and spiritual philosophies viewed the functions of our brains, including language, as energetic phenomena. Human consciousness is energy, and this energy is transformed into language by our minds (intellects). Why are there so many contradictions and inconsistencies in the language arising from the intuition? And how do the patient and the healer communicate during healing?

A Larger Picture

After contemplating possible explanations for these puzzles, I did a thought experiment: *What if there weren't any contradictions or paradoxes? Could I construct a paradigm for healing that would bring all these apparently conflicting ideas together, unifying the ideas into one larger picture?*

Considering this opened me up to new possibilities. Perhaps there was an explanation for how healers can know information about which they haven't previously been informed. Perhaps the healer's training did not ultimately hold the healing wisdom.

Before I could construct a unified paradigm between science and spirituality, I had to resolve the many contradictions among the ways different practitioners described energy and the etheric body. I found that explanations on the theories of bioenergy were inconsistent from one healing system to another. Each system has its own well-developed theory on how energy is organized in the human body, its own therapeutic methods to heal disruptions of the normal energy flow, and a unique physiology and anatomy of the etheric body. For example, homeopaths refer to a *vital force* within our bodies and claim that our vital force responds to homeopathic medicines created with the same energy vibration of the diseased bioenergy. Chinese medicine talks of chi flowing through meridians and treats imbalances or blockages with acupuncture. Practitioners of yoga call the energy of life *prana* and state that the seven vital energy centers, or *chakras*, are the source of health and disease. So why are there so many explanations for the same healing energy? It could be that the explanations vary due to language and cultural differences, but I felt that the descriptions have not changed over many centuries and varied much more than the description of our physical bodies.

I looked for a resolution to this paradox. It appeared that knowledge of a particular system of healing did not ultimately hold the source of healing. There had to be another way to find the source, maybe by looking at what is common in all healing.

BASICALLY ENERGY

Using meditation to focus my thoughts on these puzzles, my intuition (or "sixth sense") told me that energy and the etheric body could be used as a general context to explain the great variety of healing systems. Energy either supports health or detracts from health, and any healing system that improves energy flow will enhance health.

The omnipresence of energy was an integrating factor that enabled most of the apparent inconsistencies and contradictions among healing systems to disappear. The differences in terminology are just minor variations of the underlying theme that all life is basically energy and that good health is a manifestation of balanced energy.

If energy was the universal integrating factor in health, disease, and healing, then what was showing up in the different systems? Since energy underlies life, all health, and disease, was it possible that only the expression and interpretation of this energy varies?

UNIQUE ENERGETIC EXPRESSIONS

This idea felt good—that every individual is unique in his or her expression of health and disease, and each healer has a unique interpretation of the expressed energy, predetermined by his or her experience and training. These variations in expression and interpretation struck me as a key element in uncovering the mysteries of healing. Healing was no longer solely determined by the healer.

But a question remained: if energy is a universal integrating factor in health, disease, and healing, then what is the basis for the distinctions between the different systems?

Pivotal Points

Since energy underlies all life, including health and disease, it is possible that it is the *interpretation of the energy* that varied from healer to healer and from system to system. This idea felt right. Indeed, I felt my soul resonated with the idea that every individual healer has a unique way, predetermined by his or her experience and training, of interpreting the energy expressed by the person in need of healing.

The variations in the interpretation of the patient's basic energy struck me as a key element in uncovering the mysteries of healing. The healer's energetic analysis of the patient appeared superficial to the patient's basic energy. It is analogous to a group reading a book, and each reader has a different interpretation of the theme of the book. Another example is when we look at a physical object. We see the object and not the source of the light shining on the object. We see a tree, and do not look for the source of our vision, which is the sun.

This understanding led me to the revelation that each person in need of healing is also unique. His or her uniqueness is seen in the way his or her energy expresses itself. Perhaps the inherent energy of a person needing healing was an integrating factor. Conceivably, healing was no longer solely determined by the healer. These epiphanies triggered a new series of thoughts:

> ➤ If healing involved more than the knowledge and skill of the healer, then what else was present during healing?

- ➢ Was there something more important, more basic, that all these energy-based modalities shared in common?
- ➢ If the expression of energy by the person needing healing was a key factor, could it be that healing arises from a state of consciousness shared between the healer and the person in need of healing?
- ➢ Could the consciousness shared between healer and patient occur in their souls?

The Foundation of the Dance

Before I knew that an unconscious relationship occurred between the healer and the receiver of healing, I assumed that the wisdom of healing lay solely with the healer. Now the source of healing could lie in this connection, rather than in the knowledge, skills, and actions of the healer. Was this unconscious relationship the common thread that underlies healing?

My intuition said, "Yes, the source of healing lies in this connection, rather than in the actions of the healer." After contemplating all my other explanations of healing, this union of the consciousness of the healer and the receiver pointedly answered my question.

I hypothesize that energy is the medium through which a soul's consciousness expresses itself to the intellect. The intellect, in turn, receives the soul's energy and transforms it into language, resulting in an expression of the intuition. This is the process of the expression of the inner voice. In particular to healing, the language arising from the soul's energy gives information that can be taken into action by the healer. I believe these connections between soul, energy, and language help explain the mystery of healing.

Discovering that my own soul contained wisdom showed me the possibility of the sharing of wisdom between souls. Souls of healers and patients could express themselves and communicate with each other. This soul communication formed the basis of the energetic relationship between the healer and the receiver of healing. There were no confines, rules, or guidelines that could predict the outcome of the relationship. Only the fact that the healer and receiver somehow communicated was evident. And furthermore, this communication was largely unnoticed or even unconscious. Other healers I spoke with did not appear to be aware of this communication. I began to see healing as a dance between two people, an intimate relationship where both partners share in the work. The soul or inner guides of both partners were the source of the healing. Ram Dass, in his book *Still Here*, tells of his personal experience with soul connection:

> At first, I had difficulty spending time with Kelly. In fact, it took me six months of twice-a-week visits before I was able to quiet down enough inside to sit next to his grotesquely deformed body without an intense emotional reaction. Then I finally met Kelly the Soul, who existed in this body, but was not trapped in identification with that

form. Once this shift had occurred for me, it was smooth sailing between us. Our Souls were able to meet in the midst of this physical suffering and find appreciation together. [1]

CHAPTER 7

CO-COGNITION: ACCESS TO SOUL

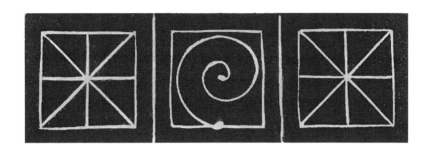

Intuition creates a connection between the healer and the one in need of help. It is the access to information that inspires and guides the healer's work.

A word was needed to describe the unconscious relationship between healer and patient. Sometimes when I ask for something, it is delivered quickly.

THE DISCOVERY

The answer came to me when I was on one of my numerous walks in the woods behind my house with my dog, Rusti. I was walking and contemplating how all the healing I had experienced fit together, knowing that soul connection was the source of all healing. Unexpectedly, the term *co-cognitive therapy* came to my mind. It was one of those moments in my life when time seemed to stop, and suddenly, life was in harmony. Co-cognitive therapy must have arisen out of my intuition because I did not ever remember hearing healing characterized like that before. After further contemplation, my inner voice said, "Co-cognition is a wisdom shared by the healer and the person being healed. This wisdom is used by the healer for his or her assessment and therapy." Until this point, I was not aware of co-cognition, its role in healing, and that it was happening in my work. I now understood, in the context of co-cognition, the applied kinesiology I was using, the hands-on healing in our healing group, the choosing of remedies with dowsing, and the use of electronic and computerized instruments to assess patients. This was one amazing breakthrough on my journey. It seems helpful if the healer brings his or her awareness to the relationship. It meant that the wisdom that carries healing energy is shared, whether or not the healer and patient are conscious of it happening.

A few other ideas came forward at that time. First of all, co-cognition does not require the healer and patient to be in the same spiritual state or even be conscious that we could be spiritual beings; it has been my experience that we seldom are. The patient does not have go through a process to access his or her own soul to make it work. If the patient is present, authentically sharing his or her suffering, that is all that is required. From my experience, most times the patient is present. I can perceive my patients' authenticity through their pain, fear, and troubled emotions. These are commonplace in my dental practice, for everyone with a toothache is genuinely honest about his or her suffering.

Co-cognition can be consciously generated in a compassionate relationship between healer and patient. If co-cognition is brought to my consciousness when I am with my patients, I can then consciously use it in my work. It would require my meditating a short time beforehand, but my patient did not need to meditate. The patient's soul would reveal itself when I was open to it. That is the purpose of meditation.

Co-cognition brought together all the ideas involving the sharing of soul information. Co-cognition is the process whereby the source of healing arises from the souls of the receiver and healer. Co-cognition explains the origin of healing energy. It also explains the success of the different methods of healing throughout the world and supports the fact that all the various forms of healing have a common origin.

Co-cognition freed my mind so I could explore all methods of healing without the comparisons and apparent contradictions that had bogged down my mind. Instead of trying to figure out the single right technique or remedy needed for healing a particular condition, my consciousness shifted to accessing the guidance available within me. The constant in all healing was the interaction of two apparently separate conscious souls coming together with the purpose of healing.

DANCING SOULS

Was it primarily the healer who guided the therapy, or was it the recipient's manifested energy that led the healing? Or was it possibly both?

A further refinement of co-cognition was born of this question, which ultimately led me to Mudryi. Again, up to this point, I believed the wisdom for healing lay solely within the healer. I assumed the recipient was someone suffering and asking for the healer's insight, seeking help to alleviate his or her suffering. The recipient asked for help, and each healer was able to heal the recipient in his or her own special way. Now, looking at the relationship between the healer and recipient, it appeared they were equal partners. There was no leader but a joined synthesis of souls—a dance of the healing souls.

Looking back at my healing experience with Hari Jot Singh and his ability to know my health history without receiving any information from me, co-cognition sorted out all the apparent conflicts around healing and became the source of healing. In this case, I was the recipient, and I can now see some unconscious force was at work.

Co-cognition is fundamental to healing. It is a source of wisdom about health and disease for the healer. It originates from the energy shared between souls—a spiritual dance with partners committed to healing. This source of healing wisdom goes beyond our knowledge of our physical bodies, our energy bodies, our emotions, and our mental states. I now understood how an acupuncturist discovered I had mono at age nineteen while feeling the pulse in my wrist: he received that information from my soul!

Bringing an Unconscious Experience to Consciousness

Bringing co-cognition into the practice of healing was the next step. In co-cognition, it appears that the healer and patient are usually unaware of the dynamics of the relationship, yet it still happens. This book is designed to awaken both healers and people receiving healing to the possibility of co-cognition. Both can become consciously aware of this communication and use the guidance more effectively in the healing work.

Upon the discovery of co-cognition, I realized that all the diverse and apparently contradictory healing methods could be understood through one fundamental principle. Acupuncture, homeopathy, prayer healing, and psychic surgery, as well as standard Western medicine and surgery could be joined into one system of healing guided by soul consciousness.

I was extremely fortunate to be involved with the healing group at the Foundation of Light. With this new perspective of co-cognition, the healing group became central to my journey. Co-cognition became the focus of our healing sessions. As I explored these ideas about various forms of healing, we were able to test each method within the context of co-cognition.

The participants were eager to try out my new discovery. We met twice a month, gathering for the purpose of learning more about co-cognition. We found the ideas that supported co-cognition were easily understood by beginners as well as by experienced healers. Positive results in our healing work were seen consistently at our meetings.

Teaching healing at the Foundation of Light brought me into contact with people who could not clearly define what the soul was and did not yet have conscious access to their own souls. Upon introduction to the concept of co-cognition during our healing groups, I noticed that the participants could easily understand this concept and connect with their souls.

In the healing group meeting at the Foundation of Light, we would divide the participants into healers, who would perform healing, and receivers, who would accept the healing. We would purposely not ask about the receiver's issue or problem. This was done so that the mind of the healer could not use any information other than what he or she received in the meditation that preceded the healing. During a group meditation for healing, one healer, Alice, clearly stated that she had no experience with energetic healing; her only skill was in carpentry. The receiver was Tammy, a middle-aged woman, who said she would like to experience healing.

There were about five of us at this meeting, and for about ten minutes we sat around Tammy with the intention of receiving information that would aid us in helping her. Following the meditation, each of us shared what we received during the meditation. Alice said she experienced nothing—no visions, no words, no feelings.

After a little coaching, Alice got that the "nothing" she experienced during the meditation actually was related to Tammy's energy; that is, the "nothing" pertained to a condition of emptiness that Tammy was experiencing.

This emptiness, Tammy would later share, turned out to be a major part of the issue that was present for her before the healing.

As mentioned, Alice was a carpenter, and it was the only skill she knew. I advised Alice to use her carpentry skills in the healing. She was directed to visualize and create an energetic opening in Tammy; Alice chose to work the area of the Tammy's heart. Using her hands with symbolic hammers and saws, Alice energetically cut an opening in Tammy's heart center. She worked a few inches above Tammy and never touched her. Alice was advised to work until she energetically felt the opening she created in the area of Tammy's heart. After a while, Alice said she could sense the area was energetically open. She said that sense of openness came from a feeling in her hands. Once the opening was gained, Alice then allowed energy from her hands to enter into Tammy. Tammy later told us that she experienced a dramatic influx of energy, and her feeling of emptiness disappeared. Seeing the influence that her actions had on Tammy, Alice was able to grasp the concept of her soul's involvement in the healing that occurred. This incident led me to an insight of what was happening with other hands-on healers who I met. While they were demonstrating their healing techniques, I noticed they would wave their hands over a patient, yet I could not perceive what they were doing. Alice's movements during Tammy's healing allowed me to see how the intuition of the healer guides the actions of his or her healing.

I play jazz guitar, and healing now looked like a jazz musician improvising on his instrument. A musician learns to improvise by studying and practicing arpeggios, scales, riffs, and chord progression, and then he takes this into his improvisations. It is said that musicians bring their souls into their music. Healers learn to perform their work by studying energy patterns, chakras, and auras; practicing therapeutic touch, acupressure, aura cleansing, and polarity therapy; and then taking this into their healing work. I observed, just like a musician, that the movement of a healer's hands arises from his or her knowledge base, intuition, and the skills he or she possesses. Healing was all about intuition and improvisation; it was soul work. I witnessed that the healers in our group at the Foundation of Light, without knowledge of the issues of their patients, would approach the patient as a blank canvas, an empty page. The healer's work would create energetic forms, similar to art and music, over the patient, using the healer's intuition and improvisation. The energies from the healer's actions would be the therapy for what the patient needed. Alice demonstrated this.

Co-cognition became a precursor to healing. While exploring co-cognition, our group came to understand that an unconscious communication—beyond the intellect of the healer or the recipient—was more significant than any particular procedure that was used in healing.

We found it helpful that healers consciously received

soul communication before they decided what treatment to use. The communication of the souls was acknowledged as the source of wisdom in healing, and it was very apparent that the guidance that promoted healing through a therapeutic action did not come from the remedy, the procedure, or the spoken words.

Guidance is found by first becoming aware of soul consciousness. Then, from the soul, healers are guided in the use of their unique skills to bring healing to the receiver. We found healers and recipients already related through co-cognition; they just were not aware of it. Even if the person performing healing is untrained, his or her actions still could be effective. This does not imply that training is not necessary; rather, whether one has training or not, the exchange of energy still can be effective. Once awareness of co-cognition is made available to healers, they then can create a foundation of knowledge about healing. Co-cognition honors the soul's role in healing, and the healer can consciously listen for the guidance of the soul. The healer can then choose any method of therapy that he or she knows to use in the healing.

In our group, healers are compelled to know the soul—their own as well as their patient's. The soul is the still point from which healing is generated. How can a healer become aware of soul communication in healing? The answer lies in a mindfulness of who we are. We can become aware of the present moment, sensing the now within ourselves and our patients. Meditation and quieting the mind is the first step. Practice is the second step. Compassion is the third step.

Soul Connection:
Symbols from the Receiver

One explanation that helped uncover the mystery of communication between the healer and recipient is embodied in an idea put forth by Carl Jung.[1] Jung states that the guidance that a person [healer] receives from the soul is symbolic, in contrast to the literal information that is imparted by the intellect. While attending a course on craniosacral therapy, I was struck by the idea that healing is a totally creative practice. It uses symbols to direct the healing to action. Whatever we know about healing (our techniques) is there to put the healing into action. However, our methods are not the source of the healing. Intention has priority over the procedure. In co-cognitive healing, the procedure follows the guidance received by the healer from the soul of the recipient.

I participated in a class on craniosacral therapy. The instructor, Dr. Clyde Ford, described a circumstance in which healing took place in an unconventional manner. What he said I would later discover, was an important key to the work of co-cognition. He stated that a woman came to his chiropractic office complaining of pain in her back. She specifically described the pain: "like a knife sticking in my back!" Instead of going to his usual methods of chiropractic therapy, the idea came to him that he should remove the knife. He told the patient to lie on her stomach, and she directed him to the location of the "knife." After finding the location, he held his hands in a position that assumed that he was holding the knife in his hands. He then gently "pulled the knife out," and as he did, the patient's pain disappeared. He had not physically touched the patient. It struck me at that instant that healing could be a totally creative practice. Seeing that Dr. Ford used a symbolic knife in his patient's back to direct his healing actions, I resolved that a healer uses symbols to direct their healing. What a healer is trained for complements the healing, however their specific skill or training is not the source of the healing. Consequently, the intention in healing could have precedence over the method.

Dr. Clyde Ford's discovery about symbolically removing a knife from his patient's back points toward a creative force, a creativity arising from a world of symbols. The connection between creativity and symbolism is found in an article by Krystyna Nowak-Fabrykowski called "Symbolism, Creativity and Learning."[2] She states,

> The interdependence of the two processes, symbolism and creativity, is strong because one cannot exist without the other. Creation is not possible without the use of symbols. Language, pictures and all forms of art are based on symbol. A person's capacity to symbolize defines their creativity simply because the process of thinking is based on symbolism.

This is demonstrated beautifully in Dr. Ford's work. The symbol of a knife in the back of his patient inspired his creative action in the treatment of her back pain.

In co-cognition, symbols require translation into meaningful data. This is accomplished through the intellect of the healer so that the guidance can be put into action. The action is characterized by the expertise each healer has to offer. Since the guidance is symbolic, it follows that the interpretation of the symbolic information will vary from person to person. This offers an explanation as to why practitioners of energetic healing appear to have different explanations and treatment recommendations for the same condition and their claims of success in the treatment of the patient's condition.

As previously stated, soul is the medium for the communication between healer and patient. However, a new concept arose: in this soul-connection, an exchange of energy occurs, and the energy originates in the patient and is communicated to the healer. I felt that the symbols did not arise from the healer but originated in the soul of the patient. The soul of the patient is a well of wisdom that the healer can access through focus, meditation, and listening.

The healer receives the energy from the patient's soul in the form of symbols, rather than as factual information. And it is the translation of the symbolic message that informs and guides the healer. This was observed in the use of co-cognition at our healing group and was demonstrated time and time again. The healers would sit in meditation with the patient and be aware of any images, voices, and sensations that would come up in their consciousness. For example, there was a visiting healer at the Foundation of Light who spoke of her methods of healing, including using her intuition. She went around the room, addressing what she saw in each participant. When it was my turn, the healer said only that my left ear seemed enlarged. She said nothing else. There was nothing wrong with my ear or my hearing at that time, but I had had an incident as a teenager when a firecracker was pointed at my left ear and exploded right into it. It affected my hearing, causing distortion with loud sounds. However, I was having no current problems with my ear. Instead, I looked for another meaning in what she said to me. The message was symbolic. The meaning I gave to the message was that I had an abundant capacity to listen. I have taken on this attribute in my work. How did this healer know this about me? The only thing I can say is that I told her through our soul connection.

Another time, I was participating in a healing class, and after meditation, the leader said he saw something about my jaw. I'd had surgery in my jaw a few years earlier that left me with some residual numbness. How did he know this? I felt that our souls had communicated, and my soul told him. The physical condition of my jaw was stable and had healed; the message I received was symbolic. It felt that it was about my holding back from speaking about my personal life and that I should open up. I used this guidance for the remainder of the course.

Applied kinesiology offers another good example of the symbolic nature of the guidance received in healing. This system uses contact with the healer's hand or finger on specific locations on the body of the patient. Touching the body either enhances the energy or challenges the energy of the patient, with a resulting strengthening or weakening of a muscle pulled on by the healer. In fact, I have seen healers use words written on a piece of paper used to test the patient. Even thoughts held by the healer or patient were used in the testing. Within this seemingly chaotic system, there is an order. The order can be seen if we look at applied kinesiology as a symbolic process that is interpreted by the healers. I witnessed healers giving the name, location, and purpose of a specific diagnostic or therapeutic point on the body with varying meanings and locations. With a scientific explanation thrown out, it pointed me in the direction of intuition and symbolism.

What I concluded from this observation is that the selection and interpretation of the therapeutic points is a symbolic message and an intuitive process. This message is interpreted uniquely by each practitioner. This does not mean that the specific points and their interpretations do not matter. On the contrary, the specific points and the interpretations matter if they are put in a symbolic context. The value of the testing lies not in the naming of the therapeutic points but in the energy exchange between patient and healer, the symbolic meaning given to the test, and the actions taken by the healer.

The question is, could a practitioner untrained in applied kinesiology be equally successful? Applied kinesiology could not be used by someone who did not know the system. However, the healer could be successful, as his or her guidance would be directed to what he or she knows (homeopathy or acupuncture). The energetic and symbolic communication would be translated into the skills of the practitioner for his or her work.

THE SYMBOLIC NATURE OF THE WISDOM OF THE SOUL: LEARNING THE LANGUAGE

I have come to know that the wisdom I receive from my soul is in symbolic form. That is, the information I receive via inspiration or intuition *represents* an idea that requires interpretation. Why is this? Our soul holds truth. The truth may be explained by looking at Jung's archetypes that exist in the collective consciousness of all human beings. Our soul expresses wisdom from these archetypes. While the archetypes are universal, in my experience each person has his or her own personal explanation of the information.

In our healing group at the Foundation of Light, a question about a person's health is put forth before a meditation for healing. During the meditation, each healer connects energetically with the patient, receives energy, and intuits something about the patient. When observing the intuition received by healers during the meditation, I noticed a variety of interpretations. For example, healers expressed seeing the color purple, a bare tree, a stagnant river, a knife in the back, a large ear, a twisted neck, and so on. An explanation is that each healer has cultural experiences, education, and thinking that are unique to that healer. An archetypical message given to two or more healers will be experienced and expressed in different ways. Therefore, the wisdom received by a healer can be called symbolic—originally archetypical but interpreted uniquely by each healer.

Once a healer has sensed the energy from his or her patient, the healer translates the energy into one or more of the following forms: visual (such as color and pictures), aural (sounds and voices), sensations or feelings (such as joy, sorrow, pain, fullness or emptiness, hot and cold), and/or spiritual attributes (such as peace, justice, transformation, and spirit). It is hypothesized that the patient's soul passes energy to the soul of the healer. The messages are first energetic, and the energy is then made into forms, some of which have been described. The forms are interpreted by the healer into meanings and then acted upon according to each healer's experience and training.

Intuition	Meaning	Actions
Purple Color	Stagnation, Calming needed	Massage to move energy, wrapping patient in purple psychic or physical
Knife in Back	Stabbing pain Betrayal	Remove knife energetically Protection by shielding chakras
Stagnant River	Blockage of energy flow	Acupuncture to disperse the block

Healers are consciously or unconsciously listening for wisdom from the soul of the receiver. Healers may receive guiding messages during meditations for healing, but soul guidance also can be gathered during energetic testing techniques. Applied kinesiology, dowsing for health and disease, or any other bioenergetic assessment or diagnostic technique can source the wisdom coming from the soul.

LISTENING: THE ULTIMATE ACTION

If all information gleaned from meditation, energetic testing, or other forms of intuitive assessment is symbolic, what advantage does this have for the person receiving healing and for the practitioner? In co-cognitive therapy, healing is not only about how much the healer knows; it is also about the healer interpreting the symbols that are received. One benefit of the symbolic nature of wisdom is that it allows the patient to be the guide. The patient feels heard. Co-cognitive therapy is about listening to the wisdom of the symbols and putting this guidance into action. The process of healing takes place in the exchange of energy between the patient and healer. Co-cognition, a spiritual and energetic basis for healing, can be incorporated into all healing systems. Co-cognition brings together science and spirit, creating a bridge between spiritual experience and scientific thought. Co-cognition unites our esoteric nature with our intellect.

CO-COGNITIVE THERAPY

The use of co-cognition during healing is called *co-cognitive therapy*. In co-cognitive therapy, a healer will receive an energetic message and interpret the information to fit the healer's experiences, attitudes, and training. The analogy of radio waves may give some clarity to how the symbolic wisdom of the soul is transferred from the patient to the healer. A radio station broadcasts music and news with an energetic wave through our atmosphere, which is received by our radio equipment. Our radio translates the energy waves into forms that are recognized by our brains: words and music. We listen to the translation of the broadcast, and our culture, experiences, attitudes, and thoughts give us an opinion where we agree or disagree or like or dislike what we hear. We then act on the information by dancing, contemplating, or turning off the radio.

The energy of the soul is received by the healer and is translated into forms that we recognize visually, such as color and pictures; that we recognize through hearing sounds and voices; that we feel, such as joy, sorrow, pain, fullness or emptiness, or hot and cold; and that we know, such as peace, justice, transformation, and spirit. Because the messages are symbolic, these wisdom-messages are interpreted and then acted upon according to the healer's experience and training. A fundamental concept in co-cognition is that wisdom from the soul is initially in the form of energy. The wisdom is energetically communicated from one soul to another soul. This energy is then translated via the mind/brain/body into symbols. Then, with contemplation, the symbols are given meaning, which produces action on the part of the healer. The healer uses the intellectual concepts of physiology, psychology, energy, and spirituality to generate an appropriate action in healing

A specific example of co-cognitive therapy is found in the use of Applied Kinesiology, A practitioner seeking information from a person in need of healing will test the strength or weakness of a muscle following a challenge to the recipient's energy body. The challenge may be a touch to one or more energetic points located on the body, which have a predetermined value or meaning, followed by a test of the muscle. If the practitioner (healer) uses the results to prescribe a plan of action without knowledge of co-cognition, the healer assumes that the test results arise solely out of his or her intellectual findings. The meaning of that energetic point appears to be defined by the system that the healer has learned. However, my experience shows that the information received from the testing will vary from healer to healer.

For example, I have found that any given energetic point on a body can have various meanings, depending on which system the healer has studied. The information gleaned from the testing is initially an energetic and symbolic phenomenon; and the interpretation of the results of the testing is dependent on what the practitioner knows. For example, most courses and demonstrations show that the point for testing the thyroid energy is in the neck area close to the location of the thyroid gland. In one course, the instructor used the end of the patient's nose to determine the state of the energy in the thyroid. I tested this out on my patients and found that I could pick any spot on the body as a specific therapeutic point for testing and treatment of TMJ pain and dysfunction. The point could be on the hand, foot, leg, arm, back, or abdomen and give the same result, as long as I focused on the purpose when touching the point.

After further meditation and contemplation, I became aware that co-cognition unfolded the following explanation, *the recipient defines the energetic point based on the guidance he or she needs to give to the healer.* The test results will give the healer specific information that the healer can use to help that person heal. The information will only include what the healer knows. This is why the results of testing a specific point will vary from practitioner to practitioner, and therefore, so will the assessment and therapy. Again, co-cognitive therapy is the result of the relationship between a particular receiver and a particular healer. An additional concept was discovered: the soul of the recipient knows the capabilities of the healer and will direct the healer to the specific points that will give the healer the information he or she needs about the recipient's suffering. The healer is guided by the soul of the recipient so that he or she can use his or her finest—and thus, most appropriate—skills for the person in need of healing.

A REVIEW OF CO-COGNITION

Co-cognition is the joining of souls with the intention of healing, and this may be a conscious process, but it is mainly an unconscious process. When healers are educated on the soul nature of healing, co-cognition will become a conscious process. The symbolic nature of the wisdom of the soul and healing creates the following possibilities:

➢ All wisdom from the soul is energy, which is processed and translated by the healer into intellectual meaning.

➢ What you have to offer (i.e., skills) as a healer at any moment is what you need. There is no immediate need to look any further than who you are and what you can do to help the patient.

➢ Souls communicate in an energetic and symbolic medium, which is why the interpretation of soul wisdom varies.

➢ Your interpretation of the symbols has priority over what you know.

➢ The soul of the one receiving healing knows the capabilities of the healer.

➢ The exchange of healing energy occurs to and from the healer and the one being healed. This makes it possible for the healer to benefit as well.

➢ Come into practice with a beginner's mind. Leave all you know behind, and be open to receiving guidance from soul. There will be plenty of time later for contemplation.

CO-COGNITION AND MINDFUL COMPASSION

Compassion can be one of the attributes that distinguishes a healer from someone who is delivering health care. You likely have experienced compassion during a visit to your health care provider, and compassion has made a difference in your experience. When compassion is lacking, our experience of health care is diminished. When present, it opens the door to a relationship that gets to the core of our suffering. In my dental practice, I am constantly in the presence of people in pain. I found that compassion allows me to be sensitive to their suffering and to their subtle energies. And in compassion, my energy is not drained; it connects me with my patients in ways that make them feel calm and that they can trust our interaction.

Compassion is also something that we, as patients, look for when seeking service. The next step on my journey was developing a compassionate mind in healing.

CHAPTER 8

THE COMPASSIONATE MIND:
THE ULTIMATE LISTENER

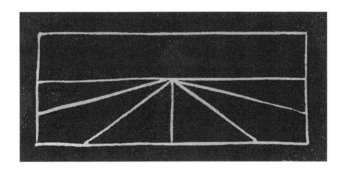

Out beyond ideas of wrongdoing and right doing,
there is a field. I'll meet you there.
When the Soul lies down in that grass,
the world is too full to talk about.
Ideas, language, even the phrase each other
doesn't make any sense.
—Rumi

I first became aware of the possibility of a different way of serving patients while I was in dental school. My awareness arose from a feeling that something was missing. The dental school curriculum had a focus on developing my technical skills. My relationships with patients received some attention but nothing significant. One day—to my surprise—one of my teachers, Dr. George Pryles, mentioned empathy. He made a distinction between empathy and sympathy. "Empathy is listening to patients and understanding their complaints from their point of view," he said. "Sympathy is feeling sorry for the patient, and sympathy may not come from the patient's point of view."

While I was inspired by Dr. Pryles's comments, I was struck even more by the lack of attention my other teachers gave to the personal side of patient relations. In fact, I remember many classroom discussions portraying the patient as a potential enemy. The enemy could and would sue us. At the same time, there was an increase in lawsuits and liability insurance costs. In our society, the cost of lawsuits and their prevention is staggering.

· · · · · ● ● ● ● ● ◉ ● ● ● ● ● · · · ·

Pema Chodron writes,

> Compassion is not a relationship between the healer and the wounded. It's a relationship between equals. Only when we know our own darkness well can we be present with the darkness of others. Compassion becomes real when we recognize our shared humanity.[1]

Many of us choose to be thrown into situations that challenge us and train us how to live in a complex society. For me it was dental school. In the context of these challenges, did I really have a choice in how to be with my patients, and would it make a difference? I believe I do have a choice. What I took from Dr. Pryles's message was that it may take discipline and constant awareness to break out of habitual patterns of indifference. I could set my sights on a compassionate way.

In an article published by ScientificAmerican.com, "The Neuroscience of Meditation," Ricard, Lutz, and Davidson mention compassion and lovingkindness. In their study, they discovered that meditation cultivates attitudes of lovingkindness and compassion toward other people. The practice entails being aware of someone else's needs and then experiencing a sincere, compassionate desire to help that person or to alleviate his or her suffering.[2]

Compassion is a way of being with another person's passion or life force. Co-cognitive healing uses compassion to mindfully be with the recipient without thoughts of right and wrong. The life force has wisdom, not judgment; this is just the way it is. As healers, we can choose to be with our patients with everything they are and everything they are not, without judgment. With this compassionate way of being, the healer is fully present in the space of the life and energy of the patient.

All the great teachers and leaders, including Buddha, Christ, Gandhi, Martin Luther King Jr., and Nelson Mandela, have compassion as the centerpiece of their philosophy and their lives. It is the basis of their writings, teachings, and speech. Compassion can move our hearts to be open more than any other way of being. The essence of healing is sourced from compassion, arising from our souls, into our hearts, and then out to our patients through words and actions.

In co-cognition, the healer brings compassion and tolerance to the recipient. For many of us, this is no easy task. It may take time to develop the skill and discipline to be with the patient unconditionally. Having empathy, understanding the passion of healing, and connecting to the wisdom of soul begins with listening in an unconditional manner. Listening creates a place for the compassionate mind to show up.

The Reverend Allen Wells writes that an attribute of the compassionate mind is a consciousness that healers can strive for. Compassion lays the framework for healing and promotes the flow of healing energy. Compassion brings co-cognition into our consciousness.

The compassionate mind is the mystical mind, or the sacred mind; it balances the innocence of faith and the objectivity of reason with the intimacy of the heart and the awe of everything that is beyond our expectations.[3]

Reverend Allen creates a context where compassion is a conscious attribute. This offers an explanation of the state of consciousness that healers should bring to their patients. It offers a way of being in which healers can relate with the souls of their patients. As patients awaiting treatment, we look forward to compassion when we are with a healer. When compassion is present, healing is supported. For this reason, as healers, it is imperative that we develop our compassionate minds.

In the context of co-cognition, for the healer, compassion sets the stage for relating to the soul of the recipient. Being aware of the compassionate mind promotes a conscious state of soul connection, and the actions taken in healing are guided by co-cognition.

Three aspects of the compassionate mind are empathy, the passion to heal, and soul connection.

EMPATHY

> *As long as our orientation is toward*
> *perfection or success, we will never*
> *learn about unconditional friendship*
> *with ourselves, nor will we find*
> *compassion.*
> —*Pema Chodron*

The first factor in developing a compassionate mind in healing is empathy—truly listening to another person and experiencing what is happening for him or her without judgment or opinion. Whether we are healers or patients, many of our experiences and relationships are burdened with conflict, the need for protection, and self-centered consciousness. It is up to us as healers to be aware of the thoughts that we bring into healing, leave behind our judgments and opinions, and choose the way of compassion.

Can you hold yourself responsible for all your thoughts,

feelings, and reactions? Examine your thoughts; are they creative and productive? If not, consider that you can choose the way you think. There may be obstacles in choosing compassion, but consider it anyway. The simple act of observing what you are thinking begins to access your compassionate mind.

The wisdom taught by healers, from Hippocrates to Andrew Weil, teaches us that we have a choice in how to think. Here, the choice is to think about ourselves (being self-centered) or to think within the consciousness of the recipient (having empathy). One could say, "When I am self-centered, I think about how I can best survive the circumstances of my life, with the primary attention given to myself. When I think and listen with empathy, I am connected with the recipient."

Self-centered thinking and listening are valuable for problem solving for ourselves, but self-centered thinking gives rise to the stress-based mind. "Looking out for number one" or "Me first" are thoughts that form the basis of the stressed-based mind. The considerations of the healer are in the forefront, and the communication with the patient is hindered. For a health care practitioner, the following thoughts would be typical of a stress-based mind:

- I don't want to be here.
- This patient takes too much time.
- Money (theirs and mine).
- I can't figure this out.
- I don't like this patient.

Obviously, these thoughts will not be productive in creating a healing relationship. It feels like we do not have a choice in thinking. Underlying these thoughts are the ideas that "something is wrong" and "life shouldn't be this way." With these and similar thoughts in mind, a healer cannot fully listen to people in need of healing or engage with them and their concerns.

Another possibility is present when our thoughts are generated from a compassionate mind. The thoughts arising from a compassionate mind give attention to our surroundings with an attitude of service and goodwill. We can think that these thoughts arise from the soul and occur with a listening of compassion and appreciation for the patient. By enhancing our listening, the compassionate mind opens the doors to co-cognition and soul wisdom. One of the intentions of this book is to aid healers in letting go of their stress-based thinking and bringing out their compassionate minds. When a person comes to me with dental problems, and I access my compassionate mind, I let go of all the records, data, and experiences I have had with this person in the past.

First, I make a connection. I create a calm frame of mind with my patient; nothing else matters except my listening to what the patient says about his or her condition. Many times I witness tears in their eyes, and their voices are uniquely authentic when they speak of the pain and suffering they are experiencing. I look for the opportunity to gently make contact with my patient, and, if it seems safe enough, I hold their hands while they are speaking.

Second, I focus on what this person is saying. I'm attentive enough to mirror back what my patient has said. This attention deepens our connection. I make sure my patient knows and feels secure that I have listened to what he or she said and that I understand what he or she communicated.

Third, I create a silence within my mind. In this stillness, an opening is created so that I can hear, see, or sense their guidance. In this still space, my connection to the patient is pure and without distraction. The messages that guide me are clearly conveyed to me and direct my communication and treatment.

Finally, I put the guidance to work, knowing that what occurs is under the grace of my patient. When teaching this to the participants of the healing group at the Foundation of Light, I convey and witness that the compassionate mind generates a sense of peace and calmness within the healer. It creates an underlying trust that is especially needed by our patients. Out of the calmness, the healer can receive the guidance necessary for healing.

THE PASSION TO HEAL

I believe human beings have an innate intelligence for healing. Although many of us are not aware of it, the wisdom of soul is already present within us and does not need any more education. What soul does need is recognition by our conscious mind. To advance our work as healers, we need to learn about soul wisdom. To be conscious of this wisdom, we need to understand the role of our consciousness in healing.

In the healers I have met, there is fervor to heal—a strong aspiration to be helpful, to aid in relieving someone's suffering. I believe the passion to heal comes from our innate aptitude and creativity that reside in our soul. The story of my daughter's pain relief from shingles demonstrates the creativity and passion that can be found in the healing process.

My passion for healing comes from my innermost consciousness, my soul. The energy of the desire accumulates in my heart center, and, with focus and ritual, it is transferred to the patient. Dr. Clyde Ford's discovery of symbolically removing a knife from a patient's back points toward a creative force used as a healing ritual, and I believe that there is no creative force without passion. Healing is no exception, but the question is, from where does this passion arise?

Some people desire to heal themselves and others; they inspire us to become healers. Healers want to end suffering, and they stand for the well-being of others. This desire could be understood as an instinctive trait—for example, a mother's desire to protect her child. But this does not fully explain the desire of healers to aid those who have no blood relation to them. It could be for the survival of our community, but healers are devoted to the well-being of everyone in the world. To understand a human being's desire to heal, we must look at the contribution of our souls.

Passion is part of compassion, and that passion arises

from our compassion during healing. Passion in healing originates from soul; this desire of soul is an energetic force with a purpose for healing. Jon Kabat-Zinn writes about passion as if it is an attribute of our souls.

> The most important support for mindfulness practice comes from the quality of your motivation. No amount of outside support can substitute for a quiet but determined passion for living life, every moment of it, as if it really mattered, knowing how easy it is to miss large swaths of it to unconsciousness and automaticity and to our deep conditioning. That is why it is important to practice as if life depended on it. It does.[4]

When a healer meets with another person's suffering, the soul of the healer displays compassion. Rosalyn Bruyere writes,

> Healing arises out of compassion. Compassion is a genuine concern for the pain of another. Compassion reflects a desire for the surcease of someone's sorrow, no matter the differences or similarities between healer and patient.[5]

One of the passions of the soul is to end suffering. My experience of being conscious of my soul is that it does not have tolerance for anything but freedom. Disease appears to my soul as a loss of freedom; and my soul is ready to come to the aid of those who are suffering. Soul most often needs a healer to assist with its passion to heal.

In the light of human consciousness, why we get sick and our desire to heal are closely linked. Some would do harm to themselves and others, or they are apathetic about alleviating suffering. Compassion seems to be missing in their consciousness. Healing that lacks compassion is a dead end to relieving suffering.

Bruyere writes, "Without compassion, the healer lacks the will to seek an answer, to research the problem, determine a treatment form, and follow through in what may be an arduous struggle to awaken the Soul of the sufferer."[6]

Healers that use their compassionate minds have distaste for suffering and passionately long to relieve the world and its inhabitants of the suffering that accompanies pain and disease.

Bruyere writes, "The healer uses ritual to create a focus of attention, to move out of the personal into the transpersonal, and trigger or reinforce the compassionate response."[7]

SOUL CONNECTION

Connecting with the soul begins with turning on a switch. The switch turns on a feeling of total presence in the moment. This is followed by a total body experience of lightness and openness. As Rumi says, it is a place without right or wrong. From this space, a compassionate mind arises, and healers generate their healing.

From my experiences in the Foundation of Light healing group, the information we receive from the soul connection is symbolic. The wisdom comes to the healer in words, forms, colors, and sensations. The healer interprets these symbols and uses the information to guide him or her in healing. I have found consistently that success in healing improves when healers access their souls and connect with the soul of the recipient.

Lois was a participant at one meeting of the healing group. She was a practitioner of massage therapy and had experience with hands-on healing. She had no experience with co-cognition. After a short meditation to connect with a patient lying on the floor in front of her, Lois received a vision that something was stuck in the patient's left shoulder area. Lois had little experience in using her skills based on her intuition. I told Lois that the patient's soul knew what her skills were, and I coached her to use her massage skills on the patient. She knelt over the patient and moved her hands as she would to relieve a shoulder that had a limitation of movement. The patient later informed us that there was no restriction in her left shoulder. We could intuit that the movement of Lois's hands physically in contact with the patient's shoulder interacted with the patient's energy field, creating swirls of energy and energetic pressures in the area of her left shoulder. Following Lois's treatment, the patient reported that the healing procedure had helped her. She had been feeling under a lot of stress, and her body felt tight. Now she experienced a feeling of calmness, of being at peace, and was ready to return to her life better able to handle her stress.

The emphasis in our group was to begin with listening. The key word here is "listen," for it implies more than listening to or for a voice. I consider that there are varying manners in which a person can be in touch with his or her soul. Some healers, like me, receive guidance in the form of words—but not spoken words. The words come out of the stillness that is created during our meditation. I consider this the inner voice or the voice of the soul. When information received is in the form of language, words, sentences, and stories, this is called *clairaudience*.[8]

Other participants perceived the guidance from the soul as pictures, visions, scenes, and colors, which are symbols requiring interpretation by the intellect to inspire their healing techniques. This is called *clairvoyance*.[9]

Some perceived their feelings. It was not an emotional response but included the emotions. It could be expressed by joy, grief, sadness, fear, or worry. But more likely, the healer would feel a sensation such as coolness or heat, a vibration, or a sense of energy. This is called *clairsentience*.[10]

Finally, others just knew—like I know in my heart; I know in all my being. This is referred to as *claircognizance*.[11]

In our group, we found that it was important that each healer discover how he or she "listens."

As healers, we then take action on the possibility that we have created. This is done under the guidance of soul connection. The action we take is from our own personal and unique way of healing. It may involve hands-on healing, guidance with storytelling, nutritional guidance, homeopathic remedies, or many other ways. Through our actions, we guide the recipient on a journey through his or her disease that makes it meaningful.

BRINGING COMPASSION

Being in the compassionate mind is a meditative state. Our pulse rate slows, our blood pressure lowers, and our sense of being is wholly with the person in need of healing. Extraneous information does not enter into the compassionate mind. Through our intuition—the sixth sense—we become aware of co-cognition and receive the guidance from the soul.

Ricard, Lutz, and Davidson write,

> To generate a compassionate state may sometimes entail the meditator feeling what the other person is feeling. But having one's emotions resonate empathetically with the feelings of another person does not by itself suffice to yield a compassionate mind-set. The meditation must also be driven by an unselfish desire to help someone who is suffering. This form of meditation on love and compassion has proved to be more than just a spiritual exercise. It has shown potential benefit for health care workers who run the risk of emotional burnout.[12]

The compassionate mind generates a sense of peace and calmness, which the patient especially needs. How does this happen? Being in the compassionate mind is "tuned-in" consciousness, where I am joined with my patient. Extraneous information does not enter into my attention. I can be aware of co-cognition and receive the guidance of the soul. This lays the foundation for a fulfilling experience for me and for my patient in an otherwise stressful time.

CHAPTER

Understanding Our
Consciousness in Healing

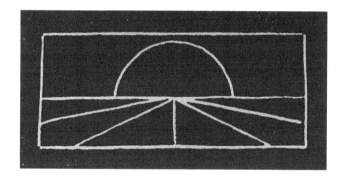

You have to go through you to get there.
—*Ira Kamp*

Alice Bailey wrote, "All disease can be attributed to inhibited Soul life."[1] As beings with soul, it is our nature to establish and remain in connection with our souls. The soul is the positive consciousness that underlies our thinking and coping with everyday life. Once the connection is made, we discover guidance and information regarding our lives that is not available anywhere else. Our souls have many attributes, including love and the power to heal. Those of us with souls oriented toward love and healing are compelled to help eliminate suffering, disease, and discontent and to promote healing.

Healing involves both the conscious and unconscious minds, working together. The function of the unconscious mind or soul in healing is to unveil the underlying purpose and meaning of the patient's suffering. The role of the conscious mind is to keep track of what is going on while the unconscious mind is participating in the work. The conscious mind also has the ability to create action from the information gleaned from the unconscious mind.

What our conscious minds do with this depends upon our individual nature and our creativity. What is common is the desire of the soul to help in the transformation of others.

I use intuition in my practice of dentistry. I am aware that not all patients are open to the use of intuition in their treatment, so I choose the time and place of its use carefully. The first intuitive tool I used in my practice was dowsing. I was introduced to dowsing by John and Kate Payne, founders of the Foundation of Light, who used dowsing on an hourly basis; Bianca Indelcato, an assistant to my acupuncture practice; and Dr. John Char, a holistic dentist I met in Hawaii. They all used a pendulum to dowse.

Dowsing has mostly been associated with finding underground reservoirs of water, but it also has been used in healing for generations. Dowsers usually use a tool as an extension of their bodies, such as a pendulum or a forked stick.

I learned that dowsing is a skill that comes from our intuition. My teachers all used a pendulum to dowse. The pendulum was a string or chain with a weight on it. The weight could be a crystal, a metal ball, or even a metal nut. The dowers held the string portion of the pendulum in their hands, with the weight extending downward. I observed that it spun in a clockwise or counterclockwise direction. The clockwise motion meant a positive response or yes, and the counterclockwise motion related to a negative response or no. I later came to know that the spinning of the pendulum was generated by the movement of their hands; their hands being an extension of their intuition coming through their physical bodies. The intuition focused in their hands and the movement of their hands were amplified through the pendulum.

Therefore, it was not the pendulum that generated the movement, but their hands. And the movement of their hands was generated through their arms, and the movement of their arms was generated through their brains, and their brains were motivated by their intuition. I consider the pendulum an extension of the intuition through the physical body of a healer.

I learned that healers can use their hands for dowsing without needing the amplification of a pendulum. By laying their hands close to or on the bodies of their patients, healers dowse or sense energetic problems in their patients. Through dowsing, the intuition can perceive and evaluate as well as offer guidance and answers to questions. Applied kinesiology, as described in previous chapters, is a form of dowsing, using the patient as a dowsing tool.

Dr. Char, who used dowsing in much of his work, inspired me to use dowsing. He used it to detect problems in a patient's bite (occlusion), to rule out toxic effects of dental materials, and to choose appropriate remedies for his patients, from medications to homeopathy. He gave me a foundation of knowledge to use in my practice.

Even though it was April when I visited, Dr. Char's office was still decorated for Valentine's Day. He was suspicious of me at first and questioned my intentions. His initial reluctance to share his work with me seemed based on medicine and dentistry's general rejection—at that time—of the use of alternative techniques. His license to practice dentistry could be subject to revocation if his methods became public. Once Dr. Char realized he had nothing to fear from me, he took me into his back room to show me the books, instruments, and remedies that he used. He seemed inspired to share his work. He had written four books on holistic dentistry, much of it based on dowsing.

The dowsing I first was shown was done with a handheld pendulum. The pendulum rotated in clockwise or counterclockwise directions. Dr. Char used his pendulum directly over his patients and asked important questions about their dental health and the effectiveness of the treatment he could offer. All I could see was his hand rotating while holding a string with a weight on the end of it. When I first witnessed dowsing, I did not get what was happening. I hung a pendulum from a bush to see if the pendulum rotated as it did in someone's hand, and it did not move. It is not the pendulum that generates the movement.

It turns out that the movement begins within the body and mind of the dowser and occurs throughout the entire body. The pendulum acts as an amplifier of this movement. Although it appeared the hand of the practitioner moved the pendulum, when I looked closer I also noticed that his arm also moved.

The string of the pendulum varied—from dental floss to silver and gold chains. The weights were a metal nut, crystals, or metal bobs. Some practitioners feel that the composition matters in the effectiveness of the pendulum during dowsing, but with so many opinions on the makeup of the pendulum, I concluded it did not matter.

I began to use dowsing to predict the negative and positive poles of a magnet. I found I could determine the polarity more times than not with the use of the pendulum. From there I dowsed for the quality of foods and chose remedies for acute conditions that my family or I was experiencing, based on the results of my dowsing.

My assistant Bianca would dowse over the acupuncture patients to show me where the energy of the patient's body needed support. I would then place the needles in locations that corresponded to what Bianca discovered. Bianca became the conduit for the healing guidance she received from the patient and then guided me in the actions I took.

Dowsing gives me the ability to access my own and my patient's unconscious mind, more specifically our superconscious mind, where the wisdom that underlies all healing resides. I have come to know that dowsing, in whatever form it takes, is a repeatable method of accessing the wisdom of the soul. All that is left for me to do is to interpret the symbols I receive into the actions that promote healing for my patient.

Jung states that the quality of our mental health depends upon a healthy relationship between our conscious and unconscious minds. Taking this a step further, healing requires a balance between the healer's conscious and superconscious minds. This then allows for a synergistic relationship between the healer's superconscious mind and the superconscious mind of the patient. This is what I found to be the foundation of healing on my journey to Mudryi.

LIFTING THE VEIL OF CONFUSION

In my healing work at my dental office and at the Foundation of Light, I have noticed three obstacles to understanding and practicing compassionate healing. These difficulties inhibit me from becoming fully compassionate and distract me from the focus I need to be present with my patient for co-cognition to happen.

The three obstacles are as follows:

> ➢ The experience of failure
> ➢ Taking on complexity as a source for credibility
> ➢ Lack of discipline

Whether you are just beginning to practice or are a healer motivated to improve your practice, identifying and letting go of these obstacles will make a difference in your practice.

Consider the first obstacle, failure.

There is a story about a student who came to his teacher, a Buddhist monk, and asked for the secret to having wisdom. The teacher replied, "Good judgment is the secret to having wisdom." The student then asked, "How do I get good judgment?" The teacher replied, "You can get good judgment through experience." The student then asked, "How do I get experience?" The teacher replied, "Bad judgment."

The monk makes a good point in that it takes failure to get us to wisdom. It is our resistance to accepting failure that keeps us from wisdom. In actuality, then, failure is not in the way; rather, our reaction to failure creates the obstacle. Failure may be part of life, but when dental procedures, acupuncture, remedies, and nutrition guidance do not help my patients, it is very disheartening for me. When patients at our healing group do not respond to our energetic therapies, we become discouraged. Failure is painful for me, and I can imagine it is also difficult for other healers. Because of this pain, I believe we spend much of our time trying to avoid failure. Although failure has been part of scientific investigation, it feels like failure should not happen. Failure was presented in dental school as something that had little value, and I worked very hard at steering clear of anything that did not have a very good chance of succeeding. My patients' health and my graduating from dental school depended on my averting failure.

In practice, the scenario goes like this: Right from the start, failure was in the spotlight in the connection between me and my patients. I had to—and still do—bring consent into my practice. To gain the consent of my patients, I must inform them that the results are not guaranteed. My patients, on the other hand, bring their hopes and expectations of pain relief, the removal of the decay from their teeth, and gaining a better appearance when they smile. This is my experience, and I assume it is the same for other practitioners.

So how can we choose to practice within the risk of failure and create an environment of compassion and healing? One possibility is to face failure in the light of opportunity. When my work as a dentist fails to make a difference for my patients, two choices become apparent: (1) to give up or (2) to examine what happened and learn to make adjustments. Within the second choice, I created an opening to transform my failures into opportunities, improve my skills, and find new techniques that could help my patients.

For my patients, dental disease, which might be seen as failure, can become an opportunity for transformation of their awareness about the health of their mouths. They can become conscious of the cause of their disease, such as poor oral hygiene or consuming foods that are unhealthy, and make the necessary changes. In light of the failures in their dental health, my patients can become aware and improve their oral hygiene and diet. They have the opportunity to return to health.

In times when there is no guarantee of success, there can be motivation to use co-cognition. We can choose soul consciousness in our work and be guided. In this way, we are capable of lifting the veil of confusion in our healing. We find a place where we can be confident in our work. Our patients become our guides.

The second obstacle is the overly complicated presentation of healing theories that muddy the water for those learning about healing. Some people just like to make things complicated. Creating complex theories is linked to credibility. In fact, complexity fosters credibility in our society. The computer world is full of complexity. But in the face of complexity, we can create simplicity. The following excerpt from *How to Say No without Feeling Guilty*,[2] portrays this idea:

> Almost twenty years ago, I met an honest, gutsy man. Joe was a young professor then and I was one of his students. He taught psychology in a tough, opinionated, open style. He left his students none of their naïve notions about the discipline of psychology. He refused to give the expected explanations for morbidly interesting aberrations or even for mundane formalities of the human mind, behavior, or motivating spirit. In place of complicated theories on why we behave in a certain way, he stressed simplicity. For him,

it was enough to describe how things worked psychologically, and that they did work, using simple assumptions, urging us to let it go at that. He held the firm scholarly belief that 95 percent of what is pandered as scientific psychological theory is sheer garbage and that it will be a long time before we really know our basic mechanics well enough to explain completely most of what we see....

Longwinded technical or mystical explanations are often intriguing and even literary, but not only are they unnecessary, they actually complicate without adding a jot to our understanding. To use what psychology does have to offer, it is more important to know what will work, not why it will work.

For example, in treating patients, I find that it is typically useless to concentrate a lot on why a patient is in trouble; that tends to be academic and can go on for years with no beneficial results. It may even be harmful. It is much more beneficial to concentrate on what the patient is going to do about his or her behavior rather than to understand why he or she behaves as he or she does!

Failure and complexity are part of our experience. They can be obstacles that are difficult to overcome and hold us back in our understanding and healing. Meditation and compassion are helpful in living with failure and complexity. In meditation, we can acknowledge that failure and complexity are present; we can allow these obstacles to be there and not push them away; we can just stay with them. We can sit with the confusion created by failure and complexity without taking action to get out of it. The result will be quietness and composure that enhance our understanding and healing.

The third obstacle is the lack of discipline. To achieve mastery in life, discipline is required. My training in dentistry was very stressful, and sometimes I felt an almost unbearable pressure to succeed. I experienced failure and discouragement and was mentally, emotionally, and physically worn out. There were several times I considered leaving dentistry and even went as far as considering dropping out and enrolling in a graduate program in biology at Emory University. I could not feel any inspiration from the dentists who were teaching or from my fellow students. My discouragement swelled when a fellow student and good friend became paralyzed after a fall from a horse. He would not recover and had to leave dental school. I was heartbroken. I was in a hole and felt stuck.

With meditation, I faced the effect that being in a hole had on my life. I had created a life without hope. Then I remembered my inspiration: To be of service to people. Dentistry was the way I had chosen. I stayed in school. I had to adjust my life. I chose to be disciplined, dug in, and continued my training.

My attraction to leaving my dental training was the

possibility of an easier way—a life that was undemanding, painless, and apparently trouble-free. As it turned out, there would be no easy way for me. I chose a life with meaning and purpose. It would be challenging and require discipline.

Human beings have a common trait that fosters the idea of making life as easy as possible, but this can be an obstacle that makes life more difficult later. For example, if the discipline of excellent oral hygiene is not practiced daily, the risk of dental disease is high. Many of my dental patients were of the opinion that oral hygiene practiced once a week would suffice. This leads to a future full of dental treatment. Who wants that?

Some of my patients, instead of practicing prevention, go the way of no action, avoiding dealing with their health because it is too hard; and takes too long, and they forget. They eat the wrong foods, are delinquent in personal hygiene, and do not exercise.

Why do we human beings forgo maintaining our health? One explanation that I have found from listening to my staff and patients is the desire to make life easy—making it easy, even if means that our health deteriorates. Most things in life that have value require a discipline that takes effort in breaking through old paradigms and ways of living. From brushing and flossing every day to the mastery of running a dental practice based on excellence, it takes discipline. As Alice Bailey says, disease and healing are rooted in our unawareness. We can choose that the meaning and purpose of disease is to push us to transform—to become aware. It takes discipline to heal.

How do we, as healers and patients, move past these obstacles? First, we create an awareness of being present. Second, we can change the way we look at the failures and complexities that arise, seeing them as opportunities for growth and healing. Meditation, study, and practice are recommended to keep on the path of enlightenment and healing. Discipline naturally arises out of the practice of meditation. The ability to focus without the distraction of obstacles is the ultimate goal in lifting the veil. Third, we can say, "Where there was once a veil of confusion now is a clearing." Functioning out of a clearing that arises through meditation and co-cognition allows the soul to be consciously involved in the healing.

Co-cognition offers a unique way of connecting the healer and patient. It creates compassionate consciousness. It accepts failure as a possibility for transformation, and it looks past the inherent ways that human beings avoid discipline and enlightenment to see the true way of healing. Co-cognition connects us with the soul and makes available healing energy to break through the obstacles that inhibit soul life. Co-cognition offers a more effective way of healing. The healer functions out of a clearing and uses soul to guide the work. The following story, written by a massage therapist, Kellie Ryan, shows the importance of using co-cognition in healing:

Kellie was working with me on a patient. She was at the patient's feet while I was removing the patient's tooth.

I know what it feels like to touch a person
and realize that I am exactly where I am

supposed to be. I know that two people playing the roles of giver and receiver are having an exchange beyond the physical (hands on body).

However, one thing I have not taken the time to do in an overly conscious way is to let the unconscious mind of the receiver speak to me (the giver) in silence.

On April 9, 2008, Dr. Kamp reminded me of this strong and present possibility. "Next time, ask the patient's unconscious mind, 'What do you need?' Ask, 'What can I do that will be of service to you?'"

A patient came to the office for the removal of an abscessed tooth but was in so much fear and anxiety about the treatment she left the office without being treated. Her emotions were running high, and Dr. Kamp advised holding off on treatment until she was ready. She chose to come back in the afternoon and try again, hoping that she would be less fearful. She came in several hours later, more relaxed, but still had her own version of "upset" running through her body. She was willing and as ready as she was going to be.

I massaged her shoulders and arms as I would normally do to the patient while waiting to become numb. She was grateful and was receiving my calmer energy. I moved down to her feet, and Dr. Kamp proceeded to work the tooth out. The patient was noticeably challenged by being in that space. Her body tensed in the legs, causing her pelvis to rise off the chair; her abdomen tensed in order to protect herself. She raised her hands three or four times to signal Dr. Kamp that she needed to take a break and ask questions that comforted her.

In the meantime, I was mindfully holding her feet and ankles and consciously "trying" to bring her energy-focus attention down to her feet.

At that moment, I realized once again that I was "trying." I decided to let Dr. Kamp's suggestion guide me. So, I asked the patient (without speaking), "What do you need?"

Within seconds I heard one answer out of the several that I felt was the clearest. I scanned a few points on her body with my mind, located over the front of her ankles to the lateral maleolus, and then, very distinctly, I heard, "Spleen 3 and 6." Now, my acupressure knowledge is limited, but I went with my hands to where I felt the points were located and placed my fingers with firm pressure beside the indentation at the fibula and the tissue of the peronius longus muscle. I held with belief that I was responding to her unconscious mind.

Her tooth was finally extracted, and she sat up in the chair. After breathing herself back into her whole body, she looked at me very lovingly.

"That helped so much. Thank you!" she said. "And I especially felt calm when you touched this part of my leg." She pointed to the spot at which I had gotten a clear response from her unconscious mind to touch. It was not pain relief that the patient felt; rather, she felt an inner peace that allowed her to be there without fear and tension.

Wow, it worked! I thought. It was such validation that we are capable of having conversations without words. Information and knowledge can transpire simply by being present.

EFFECTIVE HEALING: MAKING A DIFFERENCE

Our healing, first of all, has to make a difference; that is, the work that we do needs to change the consciousness and heal the disease of our patient, and we have to be able to see that happen. Some see energetic healing as a fantasy and thereby assume that the results of our work are insignificant. Making a difference implies that what is happening in energetic healing is real and significant. Our consciousness needs to consistently have reality checks to be sure we are working in reality and not fantasy. This is where "making a difference" becomes valuable.

We can evaluate our work to assure that what we do is meaningful and effective.

There are four steps to making a difference:

1. Commitment
2. Creating an intention
3. Action
4. Impact

Commitment is created through our statement of who we are in the work. It aligns our consciousness with our intention, and when our consciousness and our intention are aligned, we are connected to the work and our patient in a focused and deliberate way. For example, we could say our commitment to healing is freedom. The commitment to freedom brings the energy of freedom into the work. The soul will respond to this commitment. As the result of our therapy, the patient will more likely experience freedom from his or her suffering.

Creating an intention further focuses our attention to the person needing help. It can be used to determine a positive outcome for the patient and the course of therapy, and it creates a prediction of the effect of the work. For example, for a patient experiencing distress from his or her illness or treatment received, we could create a possibility that the symptoms the patient's body is experiencing are the result of the way the body releases tension. We would guide the patient to see that what he or she is experiencing is normal. Therapy would be based around the acceptance of what is happening and calming the psyche and nervous system so that the reactions are tolerated. The symptoms could also be seen as symbols of the patient's life, and meaning could be gleaned that relieves the stress of the illness.

As healers, we then take *action* on the intention that we have created. This is done under the guidance of our commitment. The action we take is generated from our own personal and unique way of healing. It may involve hands-on healing, guidance with storytelling, nutritional guidance, homeopathic remedies, or many other ways. Through our action, we guide the patient on a journey through his or her disease that makes it meaningful and that inspires health to return.

Finally, we can observe what *impact* our work has on the quality of life of our patient.

Three possible outcomes can happen as the result of our work:

> Improvement of the condition
> Worsening of the condition
> No change in the condition

In energetic healing, any change in symptoms following treatment is welcomed. The first two are seen as movement in the patient's condition. Improvement is always welcomed. If the health of our patient worsens, it still may indicate a positive impact of our work; sometimes patients get worse before they get better. An immediate aggravation of the condition is seen as part of the healing process of moving the unbalanced energy out of the body. If this happens, the patient needs to be guided and supported.

If there are no discernible changes, and we have not made a difference, reevaluation is needed, and other possibilities need to be created.

HEALING MEDITATIONS AND GROUP HEALING

Meditation can be the basis for all methods of healing, from prayer and the laying of healing hands to surgery. Our techniques are enhanced by the centering and awareness that occurs with the practice of meditation. When we connect with our souls through meditation, a context is created where the exchange of energy can benefit both healer and the one receiving healing.[3]

Group healing meditations, where there is more than one healer present, are a unique way of channeling healing energy. Out of the intention of the group, the consciousness taken into meditation creates a group soul. All energies are combined into one healing force, and the results for healers and the one(s) receiving the healing light are magnified. At the group healing sessions at the Foundation of Light, each participant who meditated with their attention on the receiver, picked up different messages. We found this to be true at every healing session. Although the received information varies from healer to healer, we found that each individual contribution to the soul-guided healings had a positive effect on the recipient.

Group healing, where there is one patient and many healers, works within a context that each healer offers a portion of the healing. If there are two healers, each will take on half of the work. If there are three healers, then each healer will take on one-third of the work, and so on. Each healer may have a distinct method of healing, but each additional healing complements the others. When the healers' energies are added together, it creates healing that is amplified in its effect.

CREATING GROUP SOUL CONNECTION

The soul contact in group healing is similar to one-on-one co-cognitive therapy. The distinction, however, is that in group healing, a group soul is at work rather than individual souls. The group first identifies the one(s) in need of healing. Then the healers intentionally form a group soul through meditation. At the Foundation of Light, this is accomplished by having the members of the group sit in a circle. All the healers in the group first contact their own souls by focusing on creating light in their sixth chakra area (between the eyes on the forehead). Using active imagination, the healers create light that fills their heads. When this is complete, each healer creates a beam of light extending down from his or her head into the heart. Here, the light fills the heart in a similar fashion to the head. Any thoughts, concerns, and worries move to the side, allowing the light to fill the entire space. The concerns and worries are invited to return after the healing session is complete.

When the heart is full of the light, each member of the group creates a beam of light extending from their hearts into the center of the group. At the point where the beams of light of the group meet, a central space of light is created. This can be sensed as a flame, a crystal, or a window with the light passing through. If it is a window, the healer can "gaze" through the window and gain symbolic insights into the group soul and the work of the group.

At this time, the group has created a wheel, with the body of each member forming the outer wheel. The beams of energy that extend into the center are the spokes, and the meeting place of the energies is the hub. From this energetic configuration, the healing commences.

Each healer shares soul energy with the patient. The healers receive and transform the energy into symbolic images, sounds, and sensations. Their intellect further translates the symbols into information that they use to place healing energy into action. Each healer is given the responsibility to do his or her part in the healing. Each healer will have his or her own particular method and purpose. All the parts, when put together, create one healing experience.

Time and time again at the Foundation of Light, we have found that the symbolic message received by each healer can be very similar in theme to that of the others. Following the group meditation, each member of the group and the group as a whole contacts the soul of the patient. This occurs in silence, without spoken communication between the healers. After a brief time, the healers return from soul contact, and the healers share what they received with the rest of the group.

Each healer then takes his or her turn in healing the patient. They have contacted the soul of the patient and now proceed, guided by the information received. When all healers have completed their parts, we ask the patient for feedback. We believe the immediate feedback is necessary because we are a group not only practicing healing but also studying and evaluating the process. In other situations, where the intent is not based on learning, immediate feedback from the patient is not necessary and can be asked at a later time.

Cattie was a middle-aged woman who appeared at our healing group. Before we began, we asked her not to tell us why she was in need of healing. Afterward, she did tell us that her relationship with her husband was going poorly, and she had nowhere else to turn for help. With Cattie lying in the middle of our circle of six healers, we went into meditation. This time, the only question asked in soul connection was where to be positioned when doing hands-on healing. After a five-minute meditation, each of the healers took his or her place around Cattie. Some received guidance to be at her feet, others to be at her head, at her shoulders, or next to her abdomen. If a healer received the message to be at the place of another healer, both shared the space. Our only healing work was to place our hands gently on that location of Cattie's body that we were guided to be. No words were spoken during the healing. After fifteen minutes, we all returned to our places in the circle around Cattie. We asked Cattie to describe her experience. She replied that it was very peaceful and profound. The worries and fears melted away and were replaced with feelings and thoughts of possibilities for her relationship to work.

In many of our meetings, the participants of our healing group, since it is their first time in attendance, are not aware of co-cognition. This does not stop the process. I can connect silently with the soul of the person receiving healing, without the participant's awareness. I contact the patient's soul, receive guidance, and offer it to the group in the form of questions and comments that support the patient.

I have used group healing consciousness in my work at the Eastman Institute for Oral Health. Our clinical dentists meet to review patients that have difficult dental conditions, such as severely worn teeth that need restoration. One patient, Rebecca, had multiple problems of worn and missing teeth. Her dental condition affected her confidence. As a young woman, appearance was very important, but a hard life had created a financial poverty, and she could not afford treatment. She recently had found employment, and her insurance covered some of the expenses. My connection with her soul guided me to be gentle with the other dentists and bring compassion to their lives so that any burden concerning the treatment of her condition would be eased. I did this energetically through holding the intention in my mind and using language that promoted compassion. Sometimes during our discussions, there would be conflict over treatment choices or costs. However, during our discussions about Rebecca's treatment, I noticed little resistance about creating possibilities for Rebecca. A treatment plan was developed that would help her with her condition without a large financial burden.

Group work is a very powerful and effective way of healing. The participants in group healing, whether they are receivers or healers, are supported in the process and come away with a clearer sense of themselves. Gaining a clear perspective is transformational. It gives rise to actions that previously seemed impossible.

CHAPTER 10
REACHING MUDRYI:
THE JOURNEY'S END

The essence of life is magical.
—Ira Kamp

I was speaking to my wife, Marne O'Shae, who is a physician, and she stated— with exasperation—that a patient of hers was denying treatment for cancer. His oncologist had told him that there was only a very small chance of the chemotherapy being successful with the type of cancer that he had. Marne said she felt like her patient was giving up on living, but this was unacceptable for her. She said her patient was "matter-of-fact about it" and was not troubled by his approaching death. However, she was troubled and was trying to figure out how to best help him to become motivated to live and go for therapy.

After some thought, I was inspired to tell her about Mudryi in this patient and advise her to take time to listen for the guidance. It just so happened that we were at the labyrinth at the Foundation of Light, and she said she would take this into her walking meditation in the labyrinth.

About a week later, Marne said she was able to connect with the soul of her patient. Marne revealed that she had received a message from the Mudryi of her patient. The patient's Mudryi gave her the guidance that she should let go of the need to motivate this patient, and instead, she was inspired to give the patient guidance for his transition period into death. The healing, in this case, was directed toward diminishing the suffering of her patient as he passed on.

PATIENT-GUIDED HEALING

The soul is the director, and Mudryi is the resource.

We traditionally began our healing sessions with a meditation focused on healing one of the participants. The healers were instructed to clear their minds, focus on the recipient, and be aware of any images, thoughts, and sensations that might arise. Following the healing meditations, these novice healers were able to offer insights about the recipient that clearly benefited the healing process. I spent time contemplating why this was happening.

Through my experiences with the healing group at the Foundation of Light, it became apparent that the soul of the receiver of healing guided the healer. Some people who attended our healing group had little or no experience in healing. Many of them initially came to receive healing for themselves but became interested in the healing processes and wanted to learn energetic healing.

The possibility arose that some (if not all) of the guidance came from the person being healed. Owing to the fact that they did not have prior training or experience, these unskilled healers apparently took their guidance from the recipient during meditation.

Simply put, healing is guided by the receiver. Energetic information, whether delivered consciously or unconsciously, is provided to the healer by the recipient. The healer, with awareness or no awareness of soul communication, is guided by this information. This does not imply that the various healing disciplines are not necessary. It is the innate property of the soul to communicate, to give us guidance. What we do with this guidance is dependent on our skills, knowledge, and experience. The methods of healing, whether created out of scientific research or the wisdom of generations of healers, include the tools and the procedures to help our patients and ourselves.

The soul wisdom is not limited to a healer-and-patient relationship. We can communicate with our own souls and can receive guidance for our healing. If healers are in pain, they can access the same information to help heal themselves, and this guidance does not exclude getting help from other healers.

A short time later, an opportunity arose where I could test this hypothesis.

I experienced a severely sprained ankle playing basketball. I went to three practitioners to find help: an orthopedist, an acupuncturist, and a physical therapist. Each had a unique assessment and recommended different therapies for my condition. During this period, I consciously chose to be aware of the possibility of the existence of an unconscious relationship between the healer and me. I surrendered my mind to this unconscious relationship, and I noticed the actions of the acupuncturist, physical therapist, and orthopedist who were treating my ankle. Remarkably, I could sense that they were guided by something coming from me. How did I know this? I experienced a calm and a peacefulness during the time I was with the physical therapist, even when the procedures became painful. In fact, I consciously projected co-cognition into our relationship. Being in the serenity of the moment, I knew that co-cognition was present. When I next met with the orthopedist, I could sense the guidance continuing in his way of being.

I was guiding the healer, and my awareness of co-cognition enhanced the healing. My experience with these healers gave me an experience of the unity in healing.

The End and a New Beginning

My journey to Mudryi began as a quest to understand healing. It involved years of exploring various techniques and theories for answers to my questions. Some answers came after much struggle; others just flowed out. My most important discovery was the apparently unconscious yet powerful relationship that exists between healer and receiver of healing. I knew something in this unconscious communication inspired and guided the actions of the healer. But what was the source of the wisdom?

The last leg of the journey brought me the final piece of the puzzle: the source of wisdom guiding the healer is the person in need of healing. My theory of co-cognition, embedded in a paradigm of energetic healing that united science and spirit, was nearly complete.

By tradition, during the healing meditations at the Foundation of Light, we would have the receiver sit or lie before us after only stating that he or she desired to be healed. The healing group was committed to being disciplined. We purposefully allowed no conversation with the receiver about the nature of the suffering that he or she was experiencing until after the meditation. In this way, the healer(s) could not have consciously known any information about the receiver's suffering prior to the meditation. We assumed that during meditation, the souls of the healer and receiver would connect and "chat." Out of this (initially unconscious) dialogue would come the wisdom and guidance that inspired each healer to do what he or she best knew how to do.

The soul of the patient, it appeared, would give guidance to all healers who were providing service to the patient. But the messages received by the healers varied in their content and meaning. For example, one participant was in need of healing. Purposefully, our healing group chose not to ask what her problem was. We would only connect and communicate with her through meditation and co-cognition. Following a five-minute meditation, each healer would talk about what he or she received during the meditation. One healer visualized the patient stuck in a bush, another healer saw the patient's hands bound by a tight rope, and another had a vision of hands placed on the patient's body.

We then used this information in our healing. Each healer performed his or her healing based on the co-cognitive experience. The healer who envisioned the patient stuck in a bush moved her hands over the patient so that she was freeing her from the bush that entrapped her. The healer who saw the patient's hands bound created movements in her hands, as if she was untying her hands and releasing her from her constrained life. The third healer held her hands in the same places that she envisioned during her meditation. She energetically served the patient by holding her hands on the patient's head, hands, and then feet and visualizing light energy passing from her hands into the patient.

One participant asked, "Why would the patient's soul send the healers mixed messages?" After contemplation on this question and witnessing the actions of the healers, I intuitively perceived that the guidance was delivered to the healer in energetic form, and the message delivered to each healer during the meditation was the same quality of energy. What altered was the healer's interpretation of the guidance.

It made perfect sense that the chosen therapies were unique to the relationship of the healer and the patient receiving the healing. The chosen therapy would vary from healer to healer, and the chosen therapy was dependent upon the training and experience of the healer. Therapies which once appeared disconnected from each other, like acupuncture and homeopathy, were now related as energetic expressions of the healer. Their work was inspired by the soul of their patient.

Previously what I'd seen as contradictions in the diagnostic findings of energetic healers could now be explained. Each healer receives the guidance from his or her patient's soul but it is the healer's interpretation of the guidance that varies.

My understanding of another key aspect developed from our experiences in these meditations. Up to this point, I believed the wisdom for healing lay solely within the healer. I assumed the receiver was someone suffering and asking for the healer's insight, seeking help to alleviate his or her suffering. Some people who attended our healing group had little or no experience in healing but were interested in learning about healing. Many participants initially came to receive healing for themselves. Following the healing meditations, these novice healers were able to offer insights about the receiver that clearly benefited the healing process. I spent a lot of time contemplating an explanation of what was happening. Every person is capable of healing the receiver in his or her own special way.

The wisdom of healing, of which the healer had no awareness prior to his or her interaction with the receiver, appeared to be held within the receiver's unconscious mind (what Carl Jung called the *soul*). Thereafter, the soul of the receiver became the source of all healing. The soul of the receiver contains the wisdom that is needed for healing, and this insight is shared between the healer and receiver. The sharing of wisdom between the healer and receiver is called co-cognition. Co-cognitive therapy has the ultimate goals of relieving suffering and creating peace and transformation.

My journey ended as it had begun: by my reception of the teachings that the wisdom of the soul offers. The wisdom revealed itself, from the initial puzzle brought forth by my brother to the realization that guidance is present for all of us. The wisdom was always there. I just didn't recognize it.

Harold was a dear patient, and I had seen him through his later years, including the passing of his wife. He had been having health problems, and the latest illness had him very concerned about his ability to recover from it. He had been hospitalized for a blockage in his intestines. It turned out that not much could be done to help him, and after three days he left the hospital with as much pain as when he arrived at the hospital.

He phoned me, somewhat desperate for help, and I did not hesitate to see him. I had done some acupuncture and energy work with him in the past. He came straight from the hospital. Harold lay quietly on the table on his left side. He was very still—so still that I was not sure if he was breathing. This made me very nervous, for I did not relish the thought of Harold passing on in my office.

I was holding my hands on Harold and listened for guidance from his soul. I heard Harold tell me, "If you are going to do healing work, you have to be brave enough to allow a patient to pass on, even if it happens at this moment."

Harold's guidance helped me in the moment, and my nervousness left. I remained with him for about thirty minutes, holding him and being present to our exchange of energy. Saying he felt calmer and somewhat relieved, Harold was able to rise and leave. A few days later, Harold passed on.

While writing this book, I felt uncomfortable using terms such as "patient" or "client" because they imply too passive a role for the person being healed. Because the co-cognitive connection is so different from the way we usually think of the practitioner-patient relationship, I began to search for a more appropriate term for the role of the person receiving healing, and my friend Dr. Bobkoff introduced me to the word *Mudryi*, which means a person who is wise. I have adopted Mudryi to describe the wisdom healers gain access to during co-cognition. Mudryi is a destination full of love, trust, and compassion. Healing will not be shortchanged with these attributes. Mudryi is now my partner in healing. Its guidance is present any time I call for it. So what is Mudryi? Mudryi is the wisdom within the soul of the person in need of healing.

The concept of Mudryi acknowledges that we, as people in need of healing, each possess knowledge and wisdom that is the key to our healing. Once I understood that healers are guided by wisdom from Mudryi, my journey reached a destination filled with peace. On my quest, I had explored healing via paths through both science and spirituality. At the end, I found a source of healing that embraces both science and soul. Mudryi had always been there. I just hadn't noticed it.

The new concepts of co-cognition, Mudryi, and the compassionate mind have been revealed from this journey. I am not limited to receiving guidance and inspiration from my own inner voice. During co-cognitive healing, wisdom and light within Mudryi also guide and inspire me as a healer. By engaging my compassionate mind, I can hear the wisdom of Mudryi, the one who suffers and who is wise.

Once I began to recognize Mudryi and co-cognition, questions arose. Was co-cognition a fabrication or illusion that resided only in my mind? Is co-cognition present for all people, for all living beings? If co-cognition is universal, how can we, as people who need healing, be empowered to aid and guide our healers? After I introduced co-cognitive principles during the healing workshops at the Foundation of Light, I started getting answers to these questions.

Healing took on the nature of playing and improvising music: learn a few basics and then start jamming. Once participants—even those with no prior experience in healing—learned a few simple principles, they were able to effectively enhance the life of another individual through energetic healing. Healing meditations brought inspiration and guidance to the healers. The receivers stated that the process was useful in relieving their suffering.

AN INVITATION: WE ARE ALL HEALERS

In our group healings at the Foundation of Light, the healers sit in a circle around the recipient. We meditate for about three minutes and then share our visions. At one of our meetings, we were facilitating group healing for one of our members whose family member was in trouble. There were five healers present. He stated he had no power over the situation and was feeling a lack of hope. As each one of us expressed our vision, it was clear that we co-cognitively connected with the recipient's soul, for all of us had a similar vision of water. In this case, water is an important symbol of support, as if floating and gently being supported by life. One healer told his vision as a story of the recipient's journey down a river. All these visions were spoken to the recipient, and he experienced relief and a sense of calmness.

In another instance, we had a group of four healers around a recipient who did not say anything about the illness she was experiencing. Following our meditation for three minutes and expressing what each of us had envisioned (this was done in the presence of the recipient because the co-cognitive sharing itself can help the recipient), each healer used his or her vision to generate a treatment. There was no specific order to who went first, and each of us performed a healing on the patient. The visions as treatments occurred as follows:

> Vision of a heaviness in the heart area. The healer held the hands of the recipient and said a prayer, five minutes in duration.
> Vision of a sparse forest. The healer took this symbol to mean the patient needed protection and warmth. The healer proceeded to envelop the recipient in an energetic cocoon.
> Vision of the color purple. The healer interpreted this symbol and generated the need for chakra balancing.
> Vision of wolves. The healer was inspired to howl loudly.

In this case, the healers received symbols that contributed to the recipient's well-being. The recipient never returned to our meeting. When I met her outside of our group, she stated that her illness was healed, and there was no need to return.

In Gratitude

Co-cognitive healing is based on the ideas and information about our souls and spirits, passed on from generation to generation to the present time. I believe Mudryi has been present in human culture since we first became conscious of our relationship to other people, and it remains with us.

The soul's wisdom is always there, although we may not be aware of it. Becoming conscious of this wisdom was what this journey was about. Everyone who participated in the healing group at the Foundation of Light, once they became aware of Mudryi, could feel the wisdom it offered.

Mudryi carries timeless wisdom. Historically, there have been many paradigms of healing, many esoterically based and many scientifically based. It is important to understand that all the concepts come from one foundation—our desire to end suffering. For many years, our culture has tried to separate what has arisen from science and esoteric healing. Slowly, a change can be seen. Early on in my career, I offered my patients nutritional counseling, acupuncture, massage therapy, herbology, and homeopathy. What started as unique services in my dental office now is more commonplace. Acupuncture, homeopathy, spiritual healing, and Jungian psychology are accepted by the general public. Just about everywhere in the United States has licensing for acupuncture and massage therapy.

There is a growing consensus to join science and spirituality in health care. The use of scientific technologies for diagnosis and treatment is being integrated with alternative therapies. My wife, a family practice physician, is being trained in Ayurveda and will use it in her practice. And she is not alone, as she will join many other physicians who use alternative services in their practice of medicine. The Taoists have a perception of opposites called *yin* and *yang*. In Taoist philosophy, one fact may appear to be the opposite of another fact, yet there is a part of the opposite within each. A little cold can be found in heat, and a little heat can be found in cold. Currently, I know more and more scientifically based physicians who acknowledge the existence of a spiritual force in their work, and many esoteric healers I have met acknowledge the importance of maintaining and treating disease on the physical level, including medicine and surgery.

Over the centuries, the wisdom of Mudryi has accumulated in our consciousness. What our ancestors discovered remains with us, including their wisdom. History has shown a commitment of human beings for healing and enlightenment. We can be grateful for the Buddha, Carl Jung, and many others for their contributions to the growth of human consciousness, including the alleviation of disease and suffering. Much progress in science has occurred, and much is left for us to discover to heal. What has not changed is our ability to contact our souls, to touch the soul of another person, and to use this in healing.

Many of the ideas in esoteric healing in the last one hundred years contain elements of co-cognition and its use in healing. If you are inspired to learn, the writings of Alice Bailey, Barbara Brennan, Buddha, and Carl Jung are great places to begin.

Personally, one of my most explicit inspirations came from my great-grandfather Kehoes Tanenhaus. He was a Hasidic rabbi in Europe and traveled with his family as an itinerant rabbi who moved when communities needed guidance. Toward the end of his career, he was asked to go to Israel, and he settled in Safed, while his family, who'd had enough of his travels, came to America. I was told Kehoes led a mystical life in Safed. Kehoes lived through Israel's war for independence and saw the birth of the nation in 1948. He died in 1950, two years before I was born into the world. The story goes that he lived in a cave and brought the Kabala—an esoteric method, discipline, and school of thought that originated in Judaism—into his life and work. In my teens and early twenties, I had a desire to live in a cave. I did not know about Kehoes's life in Israel yet. The desire to be sequestered was strong; maybe the state of the world at that time, with the Vietnam War going on, helped foster this feeling. I did not discover the life of my great-grandfather until I was in dental school. I remember sitting there, surprised that I had a relative who made a cave his home and that he was a rabbi! It was an epiphany, and I understood my desire to be a caveman was from the soul of Kehoes. It turned out that the mystical side of Kehoes was the origin of my inspiration in bringing spiritual practice into my life, not his life in a cave. I feel the cave represents my need to go inward and seek the wisdom that lies there.

Cave life was the metaphor, and spirit was the inspiration. It was a defining moment of my life. Kehoes has been my guide ever since.

Like my own story, history is here to teach us of the commitment and challenges that humanity has faced. History creates the context from which we can live in the present. Through history, we can learn what to take on and what not to repeat. Our inquiries give rise to new ideas that lead to the transformation of our consciousness. I have gratitude for our predecessors, for their experience of suffering and healing. I acknowledge their lives, and I hope this book gives the same to our future generations.

The wisdom of Mudryi, the compassionate mind, and your enlightened intuition can unlock doors that have confined you to your suffering and have restrained healing. I invite you to pick up the keys and unlock these doors.

• • • • • • • • ● • • • • • • • • •

Healing Meditation 5

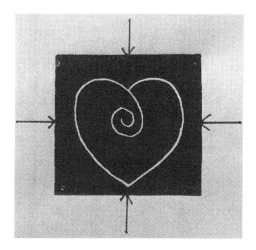

Inspiration: The knowledge received results in a feeling or thought that puts you into an act of service to yourself and the world.

Inspiration is being moved by the will of the spirit. By now, you have the source of your inspiration. It has come to you out of the co-cognition with your soul and Mudryi. The energy behind your healing work is now in place.

> Take this inspired healing energy into the work that is in front of you. Let it guide you; let the energy flow through you into the matter at hand. Stand back, and let it happen. There is an inherent knowledge and energy for which you are a channel. Let it flow, and just notice the feelings, sensations, and thoughts that accompany this experience. Notice the connection you have, and let go of anything that distracts you from this connection.

➢ The one receiving this inspired energy could be you, a patient, or a loved one at some distance away. Ride the wave of inspiration. You will know when it is time to end. At the end, acknowledge your guides—your soul, Mudryi, and the receiver. They are your source.

Epilogue

Bringing Co-cognition into the World

At a healing class I attended, the interaction between two participants struck me as a dramatic illustration of co-cognition and Mudryi. In this class, we paired up into the active participant (the healer) and the receiver. Energy work was performed, and afterward, the experiences were shared with the class. One participant, Ann, who had received healing energy from her healing partner Joyce, shared, "Although I felt energy from Joyce, and I was sensitive to the affect she had on my own energy, I had no sense about what the healing accomplished." In fact, Ann felt her experience, contrary to what one would think, created an emotional disturbance in her healing partner.

Ann had not shared her experience with Joyce at that time.

At our next meeting, Ann shared her experience with the whole group. She revealed that she sensed that her healing partner had been disturbed by her during the healing. Much to Ann's surprise, Joyce shared that the energy she received from Ann healed her from a long-retained emotional challenge, and she was grateful for the gift.

It wasn't apparent that Ann comprehended the impact her energy had on her healer during their initial meeting. To me this demonstrated the unconscious connection (co-cognition) between Ann and her healer, Joyce. Ann's energy as the receiver had had a positive impact on Joyce's life. This happened without either the healer or receiver being aware. A new possibility could be seen—that as a patient, our energy could heal not only ourselves but could heal the healer as well.

Can we be responsible for the health of others simply by allowing our interactions to occur and then observing the results? The above story would support this.

There is a world unknown to many of us. For those who know this world, it is our destiny to show those, who do not know, the way.

This book would be incomplete without a vision for the future. Co-cognition is the basis for all spiritual relationships. Energy does have an impact on our close relationships, our communities, and the world. Our medical system would benefit from the acknowledgment of the existence of soul life and its impact on healing. Politically, the relationship between conflicting nations can be improved through co-cognition.

The intellect, personality, ego, and the shadow side of life can be acknowledged for what they are. They all have a useful purpose in our lives, but when used as the center of creativity, all persons suffer. On the other hand, the soul offers the knowledge that preceding generations and generations to follow have helped in guiding our transformation.

The world's problems will be there for as long as people inhabit the planet. Healing our problems will be more efficient with the consciousness of the group soul to which all human beings belong. Dr. Seung Heun Lee states in his book *Healing Society*,[1] "Only when this system of self-worth through competition changes into self-worth through harmony will we create a truly happy and fair society. This requires evolution in spirituality that can shift the sense of what living is all about." This would include tolerance for all views, within a context of compassion, love, and the transformation necessary to heal. We need to heal. We need to transform our ideas of how we relate and support each other.

Co-cognition is a way to accomplish this. Underlying all religious and spiritual practices is a common sense that we are connected, if not by genetics then by the access we have to the soul. This does not mean defining exactly how a soul manifests in the conscious mind but opening to the possibility that a soul is there for our guidance, and its guidance can be used at any moment.

The Journey to Mudryi has shown there is a common knowledge in all methods of healing that is shared between the healer and patient. This knowledge exists, for the most part, unconsciously for the healer and patient. The healer and patient can become conscious of this knowledge through training and experience.

Mudryi is ubiquitous; it is found in all life-forms. Perhaps many people on this planet are aware of this; it just somehow missed most of us in the Western culture. However, in our Western culture, the ability to tap into our inner wisdom has persisted, despite the intellectual explosion of the past three centuries. The awareness of Mudryi diminished during the scientific revolution. Now is the time for its reappearance.

Addendum

Creating a Healing System Using Co-cognition

A patient came to my office for dental treatment and was having a hard time sitting for the procedure due to a pain in her neck. I paused for a moment to "listen to her Mudryi." Mudryi advised, "Use acupuncture—specifically, the point of bilateral Shenmen ear points and small intestine three on the right side only—and tape down the needle at small intestine three to help retain the needle." I had knowledge of the treatment for the patient's pain and the acupuncture points selected. Mudryi used my experiences to put forth guidance that I could easily follow. I followed the guidance and the needles remained in the points for most of the procedure. Gratefully, the patient was able to tolerate sitting still, and her neck felt better after the treatment.

Whether you are an existing practitioner with a discipline or an emerging practitioner, becoming aware and utilizing co-cognition will enhance your practice. As mentioned previously, co-cognition is an unconscious aspect of healing, and a health care practitioner can become aware of its presence.

It is suggested that wherever you are in your development as a healer, you should approach the study and use of co-cognition with a beginner's mind. Zen philosophy advises us to approach life in general as a beginner. In other words, leave all that you previously learned behind and take on seeing this as if for the first time, every time. If you are practicing in a traditional setting, it is not necessary to incorporate an alternative healing system into your practice. Co-cognition can be used along with your practice as it is.

Some traditional practices have incorporated alternative modalities—for example, dentists like me who practice acupuncture, nutrition, and homeopathy. This adds to the choices of therapeutic modalities that are available for the practitioner and the patient. However, you do not have to incorporate alternative methods into your practice. With co-cognition, you only need to connect with Mudryi and follow the compassionate guidance. The needed instruments, medicines, or therapies will likely be right there on your shelf or in your cabinet.

If you have yet to create a practice, ask yourself what inspires you in healing. It may be the care of your family, or it may be to immerse your practice in compassion. One of the benefits of co-cognition is that it can take the pressure off the healer to find the right therapy. The guidance of Mudryi is what is needed by the patient and gives the most benefit and least harm. The training that you had in your life has served you well, and at the present time you're never going to be more than you are in your life. It's not about getting training (although you may need to do that in order to follow your passion); rather, co-cognition is about becoming quiet and being open for guidance.

Creating a healing system based on co-cognition will have some common and some differing values from other healing systems. In co-cognition, the practitioner is aware that soul connection and guidance is part of process. The principles are as follows:

1. We approach the work with the attitude of a beginner's mind.
2. We are part of a collective consciousness/ unconsciousness of the entire human race.
3. Our individual consciousness is based in compassion.
4. We become aware of co-cognition through focus and meditation.
5. The above give access to the wisdom of Mudryi and co-cognition.
6. Begin the connection with your patient as if they are a blank canvas waiting to be "painted" with your healing.
7. Do not look any further than what you have on the "shelf" for the remedy that is needed.
8. In group healing, each participant represents a portion of the healing and collectively creates one healing system.

The goal of the book is for readers to become aware of the soul in healing, to integrate intuition with rational thinking into the healing process, and to trust the process. The objective is to become aware of this process, not to reinvent it. Co-cognition was always there. An obstacle to our awareness of soul is that we have been taught not to value and often not to trust our intuition. We can overcome this bump in the road. If we can use co-cognition to listen for the compassionate guidance, we will make great strides in bringing compassion to the practice of healing and relieving the suffering of our patients.

Your inherent abilities as a healer do not spring from your healing system; rather, the healing system arises from the passion you have about healing. To effectively aid in relieving the suffering of our patients, we need both spiritual inspiration and an organized manner in which to deliver the healing and evaluate its effects.

One of the first actions you can take in the work of a healer, especially if you do not yet have a discipline, is to create a healing system or choose an existing system to which you can constantly refer back. Personally, I like acupuncture. It is very organized, and the language has some similarities with traditional Western medicine. Remember the minds of the healer and patient need to have an organization that brings consistency so that results of the treatments can be evaluated by the healer to see if the therapy benefits the patient. Not everyone may feel confident enough to create a system from scratch. Remember someone used chakras, meridians, and surgery for the first time without learning it first. Most of us create a system by building on existing systems. Each healer may find one or more systems that makes sense and inspires, and then the healer adapts those systems in ways that work for him or her. Practitioners may also move from one system to another over time.

There are probably as many healing systems as there are people. And all these systems can be practiced using co-cognition. Co-cognition makes it possible for the soul to work within the system and guide the healer. One key attitude of co-cognitive healing is that co-cognition is like breathing; it's inherent in human healing. It's not missing; what's missing is our awareness.

The particular structure of the system can be unique for each practitioner. In theosophical studies, human nature is delineated along four states of being. There is definitely overlap and common elements to all the states, but this is a good start in creating a healing system. Conscious co-cognition can be used in all.

> Physical-based practice: medicine, dentistry, physical therapy, and surgery
> Energy-based practice: acupuncture, craniosacral therapy, homeopathy, dowsing
> Emotion-based practices: counseling and psychotherapy, music and art therapy
> Mental-based practices: psychiatry, counseling, and psychotherapy

Typically, a healing system will emphasize and deal with one or more of the above aspects of human nature.

Several practices take all these states into consideration, including chiropractic, naturopathy, and massage therapy. Furthermore, many of the energy-based approaches, such as acupuncture, homeopathy, and craniosacral therapy, do emphasize their comprehensiveness—using energy-balancing therapies to balance and heal the physical, emotional, and mental aspects. The popular term "w/holistic" refers to this precisely: using therapies to heal all levels of the human nature—physical, energy, emotional, and mental—often in a spiritual context.

A system of healing can be seen as a set of principles related to restoring and maintaining health. Each healing system has a language unique to its organization. Systems may contain various techniques and methods in their practice. Chinese medicine (acupuncture), chakras and auras, homeopathy, craniosacral therapy, applied kinesiology, shamanic and spiritual journeys, Reiki therapy, and therapeutic touch are systems that have been created. Each one has distinct methods and techniques that support the system. For instance, traditional Chinese medicine includes acupuncture as one technique among four modalities, all within a framework based on worldviews, philosophies, and theories of anatomy, health and disease, and medicine. Chinese medicine employs the methods of acupuncture, moxabustion, exercise, and meditation. Acupuncture can be practiced using several different techniques. Studying one or more of these methods in detail will give the healer a strong foundation to guide the healing and follow and evaluate the patient. Modalities such as homeopathy, Reiki, and acupuncture have the intention of healing all aspects of our human nature. Due to economic and societal influences, specialization has become the way of being in healing. Co-cognitive therapy creates a context that encompasses all forms of healing.

Another possibility is to create your own healing system. At first this may seem incredible. Originally, someone created the above-mentioned systems without major funding or the benefit of modern scientific research. With some thought and creativity, including accessing your soul, your system will appear.

There possibly are as many healing systems as there are healers. We are individual in our healing, if not in the method then in the practice of a method. All healers will practice a unique way, even when trained in a specific technique. Ultimately, it is the soul of the patient, Mudryi, that guides the healer. In co-cognition, the soul of the patient knows what the healer is capable of doing and will guide the healer within the known methods.

Having an organized healing system contributes to both the soul of the patient and the soul of the healer. Guidance for the healer is easily accepted and put into action when the healer is trained in a particular method. I invite you, as a healer, to access your passion, train in a particular method, bring co-cognition into your healing, and tap into the soul of the patient.

STEPS IN CREATING A HEALING SYSTEM

On my journey to Mudryi, I noticed that healing systems had some things that were present and some things that were missing. The common threads in all healing systems are assessment (findings), diagnosis (a name given to the condition), and therapy for the condition. What was commonly missing was the value of soul in the relationship between healer and patient.

There are three keys to healing: co-cognition, Mudryi, and compassion. They are three cogs in a mechanism of being conscious of the soul in healing. There is one more cog necessary for completion; the fourth cog is a healing system. The system can be as simple as the remedies that you already have on your shelf, or as complex as the most technical surgery. The basics in all of these systems will be defined, and examples will be given. The first seven steps include what is common to healing systems. What is commonly missing—co-cognition and Mudryi—is defined in step 8.

1. IDENTIFY YOUR PASSIONS

The first step is identifying the areas in which you would love to be involved in healing. Having passion around your path will forever inspire you in the work. Explore all the possibilities to which you are drawn and then choose your way. Having a strong commitment to your way of healing is very important. Healers go through ups and downs in their experience of healing others, and staying with your commitment is the best thing you can do. However, if there comes a time when you lose your passion for the path you have chosen, put more effort into study and learning or choose another path. Ultimately, the soul guides the healing, and the method is only a reflection of your passion for the work. Do not get hung up on a particular method; if it does not inspire you, move on.

The healer needs to choose the work that focuses his or her interest. If you are excited about the possibility of using needles to stimulate the energetic body, an opportunity with the field of acupuncture may be for you. Pursuing an education to become a professional in the field of acupuncture is the best way to incorporate the five-elements system into a healing practice. Our society has accepted the principles of the five elements in the context of acupuncture. Working with the system of the five elements also has been incorporated within the modalities of chiropractic care, homoeopathy, applied kinesiology, and computerized energetic healing systems. Many lay healers use the five elements as a guide in their intuitive healing.

2. DEFINE HEALTH AND DISEASE

The definition of health and disease varies with cultures and personality. For some, pain is a curse; for others, it is a message for living a life out of balance and points to the direction for transformation. Another example is the flu vaccine. Some people cannot live without it—literally. Others won't go near it and prefer prevention. So, what to do?

Choose a definition of what you see as health and what you see as disease, and use these definitions as your guide. Creating a framework in which to see yourself and your patients will help your soul to guide you in healing. If you are currently practicing healing, then the definitions of health and disease are laid out for you in the system. If you are new to the practice of healing, spend some time studying and incorporating the ideas of health and disease until you are comfortable. The meaning of health and disease may change during your lifetime but having the foundation for health and disease will remain.

One way that we visualize health is when the patient has no complaints. When there are complaints, there is disease. Homeopathy, for example, bases its assessment of the patient on a list of complaints and experiences of the patient. These complaints are matched to a list of complaints compiled from people were healthy and took the remedy. Their mental, emotional, and physical symptoms that arose from taking the remedy were observed and recorded.

3. DEFINE THE HEALING

The next step in developing your system is to define healing. (I shared a definition of healing in chapter 1.) Healing can be a journey for us. Each step along the way can be a healing that leads to another step in the process. Healing could be seen as peeling an onion, where disease can be hidden behind each layer. The healing involves peeling each layer away to get to the place of freedom— an uninhibited life guided by the soul. And peeling each layer is a healing. The answer is up to you.

Ultimately, in co-cognition, the goal of healing is to reconnect the patient with his or her soul and to allow the energy to flow in a way that relieves suffering and promotes transformation and freedom. The results may manifest as the relief of physical, emotional, or mental distress. The results may be a transformation of the patient's way of being, or it may be peace at the time of death. Co-cognition requires a focus on the ideas of healing that you have created. What follows for the patient is for his or her greatest benefit. Co-cognition and Mudryi give the healer access to wisdom that supports and therapies that heal the patient.

Not all healers and healings produce results that can be considered healing, as defined above. Sometimes it appears we are met with failure, slow movement, or no movement in the transformation. Does this mean the healing did not work or that the procedure was not done well? The answer to the question is in our collective consciousness. With positive intentions, the interaction of the healer and patient will be, at the least, to do no harm. If the patient does continue to suffer and not improve after the healing, we may consider the possibility that a healing crisis occurred. This crisis can be an opening in the awareness of the patient, where the efforts of the healer have set the stage for the next step in healing. When a healer is focused on co-cognition, and the wisdom is from the soul, as opposed to the ego, then what transpires is for the benefit of the patient. Healing promotes the connection of the patient to his or her soul.

4. Choose Your Tools

The instruments that healers use may be as simple as their hands and as complicated as computer-generated therapies used by medical professionals. The path you choose will make available the tools you need, and you can add more. If you are beginning from scratch, consider dowsing with a pendulum and using the remedies that are on your shelf at home.

In co-cognitive therapy, the soul is the source of the healing. The tools used in healing are the medium through which the healing energy is expressed to the patient. Once co-cognition is accepted, the fundamental definitions of the system are understood, and your passions are identified, the next step is to choose the tools you will use in healing. Of course, the simplest tools to use are your voice and hands. Most of us are already equipped with one or both of these tools. The use of guidance, counseling, coaching, touch, massage, and the laying of hands are used by many healers. Another possibility is using dowsing or applied kinesiology.

The following tools are used by many healers, and the opportunities to learn the techniques are readily available:

- colors and light
- Reiki energy through the use of creative visions and the laying of hands
- herbal and homeopathic therapies
- music and art

Remember—in co-cognition the origin of the healing is the soul. Whatever tools you choose, co-cognition requires a relationship with the soul. By working while feeling a connection to your soul, your healing will be more compassionate and less likely to cause any harm and will be beneficial to both healer and patient.

5. KEEPING RECORDS

Keeping track of your work is an important part of how you serve your patients. Through experience, you will find what therapies work and what therapies need to be put aside. Being able to look back on your work through your written records creates a valuable foundation for evaluating the tolerance and effectiveness of the treatments.

Creating a form for record keeping is a good way to begin documenting your practice. Although it may be time-consuming or seem unnecessary, good documentation allows reflection on the treatments and will give you clues and guidance on aiding the patient. A simple form can be used to note and record whether the outcome of the therapy is effective. If the treatment has been ineffective, then other modalities could be used or referral to another practitioner may be in order. The following is a simple form:

Date	Methods Used	Imbalances	Treatment	Outcome

6. EVALUATION OF YOUR WORK

The evaluation of the healing goes hand in hand with keeping records. At different points in time, it is necessary to evaluate your work in terms of how successful the therapy has been for your patients. Have you made a difference in your patients' lives?

Our initial experiences of success in healing are inspiring and exciting; aiding the healing of another person is rewarding. Then we will probably encounter people whose healing seems more difficult, and the fruits of our labors seem to diminish. After a period of questioning, studying, and reevaluating the results of a therapeutic approach, healing usually returns with some consistency. This appears to be the path of many healers with whom I have spoken. Knowing this ahead of time may make this transition period a little easier.

With proper and timely evaluations, your healing work will become more effective and rewarding

7. Continuing Education

Be committed to upgrading your knowledge of the spirit and of healing techniques. The healing professions are changing, and the needs of our patients also are changing. As healers, we have a desire to renew and enhance our knowledge of healing and the techniques. Gaining knowledge for your practice gives Mudryi more to work with. The practice of quieting and focusing techniques, such as mediation, tai chi, and yoga, will enhance your ability to be with the soul.

Studying with and receiving training from other practitioners will help maintain and improve your techniques, enhance your passion, and benefit your patients. A routine schedule of meditation is important for developing an awareness of the guidance from your soul in these matters.

8. INCORPORATE THREE KEYS INTO YOUR PRACTICE

The three keys in co-cognitive therapy are co-cognition, compassion, and Mudryi. Your inherent abilities as a healer do not spring from the healing system; rather, the healing system arises from a passion you have about healing. To effectively aid in relieving the suffering of our patients, we need both spiritual inspiration and an organized manner in which to deliver the healing and evaluate its effects. The spiritual inspiration comes from our focus on Mudryi and using the guidance compassionately to help.

Co-cognitive therapy has been described as the knowing that occurs under all circumstances of healing. We are not required to be conscious of this, but knowing that it underlies all healing creates a foundation for the healer. As individual practitioners, it offers insights on the relationship with patients. It creates a clearing for compassion, wisdom, and connection to show up in the work.

To review, first, common to all systems of healing is a sense that there is a greater or lesser degree of vitality. Alternative healers call this energy, *chi* or *vital force*. Second, a connection between the patient and healer is required, and the healer performs the necessary therapy to promote healing. Third, there is a definitive system with associated methods and techniques performed on the patient. Personally, having studied and practiced several systems, including dentistry, homeopathy, acupuncture, craniosacral therapy, nutrition, applied kinesiology, and herbology, there is no one system that does it all.

So, what is missing? We need to acknowledge that there is no particular method or system that is fundamental to healing. I propose that successful healing does not necessarily occur because the healer used the one best healing technique or remedy. Many possible treatments have the potential to heal a given condition. What is missing is your awareness of the shared process of co-cognition. I invite you to take this on in your practice. Your soul and Mudryi are waiting.

Endnotes

In the Beginning

[1] Kathy Newburn, *A Planetary Awakening: Reflections on the Teachings of the Tibetan in the Works of Alice A Bailey* (Blue Dolphin Publishing, 2007), 11.

[2] Osho accessed November 23, 2014
http:/www.osho.com/read/osho/osho-on-topics/healing.

Introduction

[1] Center for Skeptical Inquiry accessed November 23, 2014 http://www.csicop.org/articles/19990226-altmed.

Chapter 1

[1] Wikipedia Definition of Healing accessed November 23, 2014 https://en.wikipedia.org/wiki/Healing.

[2] R. A. Flickinger and J. W. Rollins, "Messenger activity of nuclear RNA of frog embryos," *Experimental Cell Research* 89, no. 2 (December 1974): 402–404, 22.

[3] Google Dictionary accessed November 23, 2014 https://www.google.com/?gws_rd=ssl#q=science+definition.

[4] Wellness Therapies accessed November 23, 2014 http://www.drweil.com/drw/u/ART03410/Applied-Kinesiology.html.

[5] Robert Peshek DDS, *Balancing Body Chemistry with Nutrition*, October 1977, 28.

6   Wikipedia accessed November 23, 2014
https://en.wikipedia.org/wiki/Applied_kinesiology.

7   http://www.boloji.com/buddhism/00110.htm.?

8   ScientificAmerican.com, November 2014.

Chapter 2

1   Physics Stack Exchange accessed November 23, 2014 http://
physics.stackexchange.com.

2   BioField Global Research Inc. accessed November 21, 2016
http://www.biofieldglobal.org/what-is-human-aura.html.

3   The Chopra Center accessed November 21, 2016
http://www.chopra.com/ccl/what-is-a-chakra.

4   Richard Gerber M.D. *Vibrational Medicine* (Bear & Company,
2001), 39, 54.

5   Dr. Harold Saxton Burr, *Blueprint for Immortality* (C.W. Daniel,
1972), 39.

6   Wikipedia accessed November 23, 2014 http://en.wikipedia.org/
wiki/Kirlian_photography.

7   *The Tao of Physics* (Shambhala Publications, 1975), 41.

8   Top Mystery accessed November 23, 2014
http://www.topmystery.com/quotes.htm.

9   *Guide to Self Healing* (Gentle Touch Healing Limited, 2000), 45.

Chapter 3

1   Project Global Awakening Accessed March 30, 2014 http://www.
projectglobalawakening.com/healing-collective-unconscious.

2   Gerber, *Vibrational Medicine*, 54,305.

3   Hans Selye, *The Stress of Life* (McGraw-Hill, 1978), 57.

4   Alice Bailey Lucistrust.com.

5   Gerber, *Vibrational Medicine*, 58.

Chapter 4

1   T. S. Kuhn, *The Structure of Scientific Revolutions* (Chicago:
University of Chicago Press, 1962), 64.

2   Boloji accessed November 21, 2016

http://www.boloji.com/buddhism/00110.htm.

3   Ricard, Lutz, and Davidson, "The Neuroscience of Meditation," Scientific American.com, November 2014, 64.

4   Pathwork Guide Lectures, an Unedited Lecture, March 4, 1960.

Chapter 5

1   Collins Dictionary accessed November 14, 2014 http://www.collinsdictionary.com/dictionary/american/intellect.

2   Alice Bailey, *Intellect to Intuition* (Lucis Trust, 1960), 73, 147.

3   Osho, *Intuition: Knowing beyond Logic* (St. Martin's Press, 2001), 1, 73.

4   Bailey, *Intellect to Intuition*, 73, 147.

5   Spiritual Science Research Foundation accessed November 22, 2016 http://www.spiritualresearchfoundation.org/spiritual-research/sixth-sense/what-is-sixth-sense.

6   Myers Briggs Foundation accessed November 22, 2016 http://www.myersbriggs.org/my-mbti-personality-type/mbti-basics/sensing-or-intuition.htm.

7   Osho, *Intuition: Knowing beyond Logic*, 76, 182.

8   Bailey, *Intellect to Intuition*, 76, 95.

9   Bailey, *Intellect to Intuition*, 76, 148.

10   Mona Lisa Schultz, *Awakening Intuition* (Three Rivers Press, 1998), 30, 77.

11   C. G. Jung and J. Campbell, *The Portable Jung* (New York: Penguin Books, 1976), 79.

12   Wikipedia accessed November 23, 2016 https://en.wikipedia.org/wiki/Active_imagination.

13   Bailey, *Intellect to Intuition*, 82, 92.

14   Care 2 accessed November 23, 2016 http://www.care2.com/greenliving/7-stories-that-will-make-you-believe-in- pg. 7090 miracles.html#ixzz3zOHgIHuf.

15 Yogananda accessed November 14, 2014 http://www.yogananda. com.au/g/g_superconscious_mind.html.

16 Heart Math accessed November 14, 2014 https://www. heartmath.orghttp://www.charlsonmeadows.org/events-library/ ways-of-knowing-events/intuition-health-healing/ research-on-intuition/.

17 Alice Bailey, *Discipleship in the New Age* 1, (Lucis Trust, 1972), 85, 239.

Chapter 6

1 Ram Dass, *Still Here: Embracing Aging, Changing, and Dying* (Riverhead Books, 2001), 92.

Chapter 7

1 C. G. Jung and J. Campbell, *The Portable Jung* (New York: Penguin Books, 1976), 98.

2 *The Journal of Creative Behavior* 26, no. 4 (December 1992): 268–272, 99.

Chapter 8

1 Pema Chodron, *The Places That Scare You: A Guide to Fearlessness in Difficult Times* (Shambhala: 2002), 107.

2 Ricard, Lutz, and Davidson, "The Neuroscience of Meditation," 107.

3 Richard Carlson, ed., *Healers on Healing* (Tarcher, 1989).

4 Jon Kabat-Zinn, *Arriving at Your Own Door* (Hyperon, 2007). http://www.ucsummit.org/Sermons/AW/20030629.shtml.

5 Carlson, *Healers on Healing*, 106, 112.

6 Ibid.

7 Carlson, *Healers on Healing*, 37, 112.

8 Anna Sayce accessed November 14, 2014 http://annasayce.com.

9 Cyrstal Links accessed November 14, 2014http://www. crystalinks.com.

10   Anna Sayce accessed November 14, 2014 http://annasayce.com. pg. 113

11   Erin Pavlina accessed November 14, 2014 http://www. erinpavlina.com.

12   Ricard, Lutz, and Davidson, "The Neuroscience of Meditation," 114.

Chapter 9

1   Alice Bailey, *Esoteric Healing* (Lucis Press, 2007), 117, 532.

2   Patti Breitman and Connie Hatch, *How to Say No without Feeling Guilty* (Broadway Books, 2000), 119.

Epilogue

1   Seung Heun Lee, *Healing Society* (Hampton Roads Publishing, 2000), 141.